Making
Fairy Folk

Steffi Stern

Hawthorn Press

Hawthorn Press

Published by Hawthorn Press, Hawthorn House,
1 Lansdown Lane, Stroud, Gloucestershire, GL5 1BJ, UK
Tel: (01453) 757040
Email: info@hawthornpress.com
Website: www.hawthornpress.com

Photographs © Oliver Perrott
Additional photography by Saskia Leljak
Illustrations and design by Lucy Guenot
Typeset in 'Myriad Pro' and 'Maiandra' fonts
Printed in UK by Short Run Press Ltd, Exeter
Printed on environmentally friendly paper manufactured from renewable forest stock and other controlled sources.

British Library Cataloguing in Publication Data applied for
ISBN 978-1-912480-51-7

Making
Fairy Folk

Steffi Stern

30 Magical Needle Felted Characters

Hawthorn Press

Dedication

This book and the projects all came together during the most challenging times that today's generations are experiencing: the Pandemic and the Climate Crisis.

I want to dedicate this book to the natural world. A place where I slow down and find peace, hope, rejuvenation, fresh air and a sense of being alive. We must look after this miracle we so often take for granted. I am surrounded on a daily basis by forests, wild life and stunning sunrises and sunsets for which I am eternally grateful. It puts everything into perspective. When writing this book I was literally 'away with the fairies' and loved it!

Contents

Introduction

As a child I grew up in the South West of Germany and I spent many happy childhood hours in the largest forest in Western Europe, the Pfälzer Wald or, also known as the Palatinate (Palatine) Forest. Hours and hours of walking through the thick magical world of fairytales and wildlife, climbing the heights of hills to reach a ruin of a castle and overlook the vast ocean of tree tops. The forest is over 1700 square kilometres large, which equals over 420,000 acres and it puts into context why Hänsel needed to put breadcrumbs out so that he and Gretel would find their way back home.

As a three-year-old I was told about the mythical creature of Elwetritsche who inhabited the forest. In my child's mind I turned this into a friendly other-wordly creature. I found out much later it appears to be a mix between a bird like creature with antlers and scales instead of feathers. I prefer how in my imagination it was a kind of fairy mixed with a gnome that lived on the forest ground and was incredibly shy and would only show itself at night. It protected the forest and if you showed respect to wildlife and nature you needn't worry. And that's just one of the things I love about fairies and gnomes – they are what you want them to be!

Looking out for Elwetritsche has probably been my first fairy inspiration and spurred my imagination into believing that there are elusive and delicate creatures that are an alter ego of the natural world including animals, plants and nature phenomenon such as Earth, Water, Air and Fire. Believing that there are spiritual forces was a way for me to find a deep respect for Nature, the Elements, Fauna and

Faeries, come take me out of this dull world,

For I would ride with you upon the wind,

Run on the top of the dishevelled tide,

And dance upon the mountains like a flame.

William Butler Yeats, *The Land of Heart's Desire.*

Flora. Even to this day I find huge comfort in the belief that there is a form of protection around the precious natural world.

As a child I took for granted the variety and vastness of wildlife small and large. I always had an insatiable fascination with lizards, newts, salamanders, frogs, toads and similar. I would spend hours at a forest spring near my home and try to catch them so I could only hold them in my hands for a brief pleasurable moment. To me they were creatures of perfection, smooth, cold and with minute details that were mesmerising.

At the age of 15 I moved to the north of Germany where the landscape and nature was so very different. I still remember the pangs of homesickness for the sight, smells and sounds of the forest I had identified with so very much. In the flat north I discovered more of the Elements of Air and Water though I must say that I feel most happy with my two feet firmly rooted on the ground either in woodland or up on a mountain. I never refound that feeling of home until I moved to the Forest of Dean in Gloucestershire UK in 2019. For the first time in 35 years I connected with nature as I had done as a child and my roaming through the beech and pine forest brought back memories and the connection to the magic of flora and fauna that I had missed so much. For the first time in years I saw toadstools again! I truly treasure walking on the bed of pine needles (EARTH) and being surrounded by total silence and a sense of otherworldliness, discovering the hidden forest lakes, waterfalls, springs and rivers (WATER), witnessing the vast sky (AIR) filled with ravens and many other birds small and large and observing sun rises and sunsets (FIRE) that can only be described as the sky being on fire. I suddenly found myself remembering fairies, gnomes, forest spirits. With a childlike pleasure and innocence I started making up little stories in my mind. Though my children are older now I feel a deep gratitude that we chose to bring them up following the Waldorf Curriculum, which holds many stories of magical fairy folk. I have found that allowing children to dream and use their imagination paradoxically prepares them for the harsher reality in a grown-up world. When my children were young I crafted many fairies and gnomes and these are coming alive again in this book.

Whatever age you are, join me on a journey into a magical world where life is filled with love and possibilities and where fairy folk look after nature and their inhabitants. Let your imagination meander and allow yourself to dream of a natural world that is rich with kindness, painted in beautiful colours, filled with fresh air. Surround yourself with natural beauty and embrace and revere the life we so often take for granted.

Steffi Stern

Materials and Tools

Here are a few useful items that you may want to acquire before you start making projects out of this book. All fibres used here are washed and some are dyed as well. I should also mention that whilst most of the fibres used in the book here are not suitable for vegans they are however sourced from suppliers where the highest standard of animal welfare is paramount. All fibres either comply with the Global Organic Textile Standards (GOTS) or are locally sourced from small farmers I trust and they are dyed under the OEKO-Tex standards (tested for harmful substances). Vegan fibres that are not plant based are inevitably manmade and are potentially less environmentally friendly and not biodegradable.

Wool fibres
Wool batts and wool tops (roving)

Natural animal wool fibres are particularly suitable for felting as they have microscopic barbs that catch and hold onto each other. In general, I work with wool batts for 3D shaping which covers most of the animals and gnomes. I use wool tops or other tops for making the more delicate fairies. The wool batts here have been carded on large industrial drum carders into lofty thick sheets and the fibres are often coarser and of medium length. There are of course exceptions! The way the wool has been processed means that the fibres are pre-tangled and they lend themselves particularly well for sculpting with wool. I use core wool batts which are of a lesser quality and are undyed as a cheaper alternative to build up the core of larger projects (such as the Salamander (page 181) and Toadstool House (page 75) rather than using beautifully dyed wool which will be covered again. For the smaller, more delicate fairies I use Australian Merino wool batts for their faces, arms and legs.

Wool tops are combed into strands and the fibres are usually longer and finer. Working with these fibres is amazing when making delicate fairy dresses, wings or silky hair (Forget-Me-Not Fairy page 111 and Sun Fairy page 127). For the larger fairies I use South American or Australian Wool tops for their faces, arms and legs.

Natural wool curls

The natural wool curls used in this book include:
Bluefaced Leicester or **Leicester curls** for their tiny wavy locks. This makes them especially suitable for fairies to achieve realistic proportions. They can be used in natural colours, varying from browns to grey and white, as well as dyed. (Seed Baby in a Walnut Shell page 67, Large Gnome page 83, Small Gnome page 89 and Wild Rose Fairy page 27).
Teeswater curls are lustrous and long. When washed they can be surprisingly white and they look beautiful dyed too (Amethyst Fairy page 33 and Ice Fairy page137).
Wensleydale curls are similar to Teeswater curls but tend to be shorter and less glossy.

> IDENTIFY THE DIFFERENT WHITE WOOLS:
> - Basic core wool: Off-white, quite 'bitty', may contain natural vegetation.
> - Lanolin-rich core: Cream in colour, feels 'sticky', may contain natural vegetation.
> - Natural White NZ Merino: The whitest wool with even fibres.

Other fibres

There are fibres other than wool used in this book that work particularly well for fairies due to their soft, silky and lustrous appearance. Some of these are less suitable for felting on their own but are perfect to be used as a cover just attached with a few needle stabs for hair, dresses or wings.

Mohair tops

From a goat, these are classed as hair rather than wool. They are shiny and have a wavy effect. These are great to turn into curls (see The Makerss YouTube Tutorial on 'How to make curls for fairies and figures). They work well on their own for hair too (Rainbow Fairy page 105).

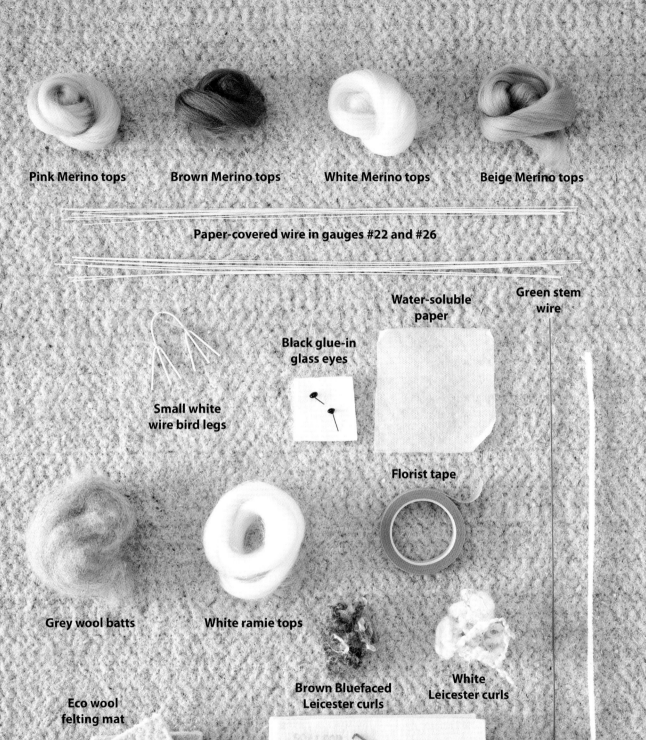

Pink Merino tops

Brown Merino tops

White Merino tops

Beige Merino tops

Paper-covered wire in gauges #22 and #26

Water-soluble paper

Green stem wire

Black glue-in glass eyes

Small white wire bird legs

Florist tape

Grey wool batts

White ramie tops

Brown Bluefaced Leicester curls

White Leicester curls

Eco wool felting mat

Extra strong white pipe-cleaner

Earth-friendly felting mat with felting needles #36, #38 and #40

Plant fibres such as ramie

This comes from a plant similar to the cotton plant and the natural colour is brilliant white, which is hard to find in wool fibres unless they have been bleached. Again, it is less suitable for needle felting on its own but can be attached for hair or a dress by using a few stabs with the felting needle. You can also mix this into wool tops easily. Other plant fibres that work similar are banana, bamboo, pineapple, SeaCell fibres and the list is ever expanding (Wind Sprite Fairy page 117).

Silk fibre

Silk is made by silkworms whilst they spin themselves into cocoons to turn into silk moths. Sadly, they die in the process when the silk is obtained, so I prefer to avoid using it. Silk fibre is expensive, very fine and adds a beautiful shiny and luxurious look. They are less suitable to needle felt on their own but work well mixed into wool tops.

Alpaca fibres

These are fine and usually come as a top. The ones used here in the book are the loopy locks which are a Boucle yarn and work well for hair (Butterfly and Moth Fairy page 121).

Horsetail hair

A great natural material to make animal whiskers (Wood Mouse page 57)

Angelina fibre

This heat-bondable fibre is used to make wings for several fairies: See Wild Rose Fairy page 27, Amethyst Fairy page 33 and Forget-Me Not Fairy page111.

Other materials

Florist tape

This is a great resource to make parts of animals that look less realistic when needle felted such as the feet of the Frog (page153) the Salamander (page 181) and Kingfisher (page 145). It is also a good aid to prepare slippery wire before wrapping it with wool.

Wire bird legs

They are a great craft supply when needle felting birds and giving the birds a more realistic look. They can be painted or covered in florist tape. They can also be trimmed shorter if need be.

Glue-in eyes

An essential to give an animal or gnome an instant twinkle in their eyes. They consist of a glass bead and a wire pin and are easy to use by making a hole and gluing them in.

Water-soluble paper

The type used here in the book is great to use as a base to make a delicate fabric (the wings for the Butterfly and Moth Fairy page 121) or to build up bulk (Minnow page 159). It can be dissolved in water and the sticky residue helps to stiffen the finished fabric when dried. It can also stay in undissolved as it almost entirely becomes part of the needle felted shape (Minnow page 159)

Wool-viscose felt sheets

These are great when needle felting flowers as the felt is strong but thin and it is an all-natural material.

PVA glue

Basic glue which may be needed at times and is particularly useful if it comes in a bottle or glue stick with a fine nozzle to apply small dabs of glue in a tiny area, such as glue-in eyes.

Silky thread

An essential if you are hanging your fairies up or if you need to sew on tiny details.

Extra strong thread

This is needed for the basic shape making of the larger fairies.

Embroidery thread

Some fairies have sewn on features such as eyes and mouth (Forget-Me-Not Fairy page 111).

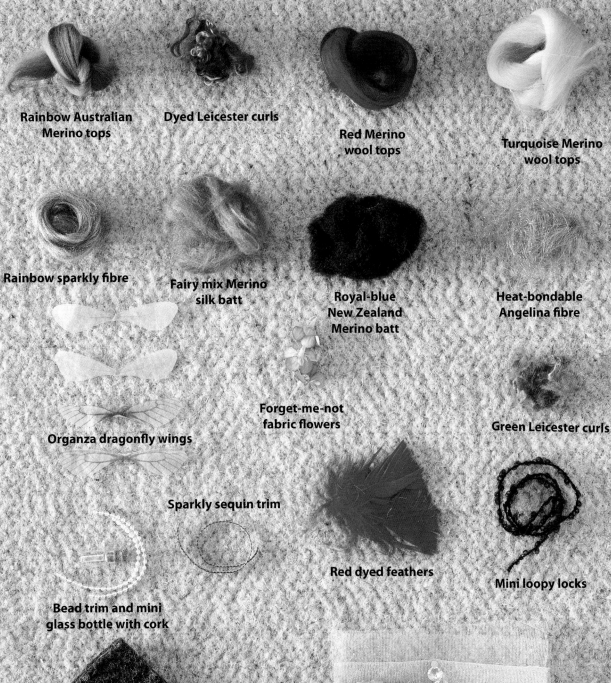

Rainbow Australian
Merino tops

Dyed Leicester curls

Red Merino
wool tops

Turquoise Merino
wool tops

Rainbow sparkly fibre

Fairy mix Merino
silk batt

Royal-blue
New Zealand
Merino batt

Heat-bondable
Angelina fibre

Forget-me-not
fabric flowers

Green Leicester curls

Organza dragonfly wings

Sparkly sequin trim

Red dyed feathers

Mini loopy locks

Bead trim and mini
glass bottle with cork

Structural core wool

Amethyst crystals and rhinestones
sitting on organza and tulle fabric

Wire

Wire is essential to make the fairies but it is also needed to make the pose-able animals such as the Frog (page 153) and Wood Mouse (page 57). The suitability of wire depends a lot on its gauge (thickness), material and whether it is covered or not.

Pipe cleaners

These need to be extra strong like the white cotton covered pipe cleaners that were made to clean pipes rather than the fluffy floppy ones available for general crafts. As they are covered, they are great for wrapping wool around. The disadvantage is that they are usually only 30cm (12in) long and if using longer lengths they tend to be less strong.

Flexible steel wire

This has been a recent discovery for me and a wonder wire for fairies and it comes in 45cm (18in) lengths. The wire itself appears to be serrated and therefore wool grips onto it really well. As there is no other cover on it, it is particularly suitable for making very delicate and thin shapes such as arms and legs.

Paper-covered or other covered wires

Covered wires come in many different varieties. In the book we have used paper covered wire which is used in floristry and comes in three different sizes: #22, #26 and #32. These numbers are wire gauge measurements: the smaller the number the thicker the wire.

Bare wire

If you are working with uncovered wire, I recommend using florist tape, a little glue, or wax to prepare the wire and to stop the wool slipping around.

Accessories

Wings can be made from many different materials. In this book I have used feathers, heat-bondable Angelina fibre, organza and tulle fabrics as well as wool.

Lots of natural accessories can be found in nature and they make a perfect match when making your fairy folk and animals. In this book we used many natural elements such as: walnut shells, pinecones, dried flowers, beechnut shells, twigs and acorns.

Decorate your fairies with delicate items and resist the urge to over accessorise them. Let the beautiful wool and overall appearance be the first thing you notice and allow the extra decorations to complete the project. Use beads, crystals, paper and silk flowers, rhinestones or other miniature decorations for this.

Tools

The following tools are essential for making the projects here in the book, so make sure you have these before you start:

Felting needles and multi-needle tools

You will need felting needles for all of the projects in the book. The needles used here are coarse #36, medium #38 and fine #40. Whether these needles are triangular, star or cross shape (cross section) is a personal choice. For the larger projects such as the fawn, toadstool house and salamander you may want to use multi-tools with three or more needles. Using these speeds up the needle felting process and again is a personal choice.

Felting mat

I urge you to use an environmentally friendly felting mat. The Earth-Friendly felting mat as well as the Eco wool mats used in the book are made from wool and can be composted at home when no longer needed. Foam or other plastic felting mats are usually non-recyclable and non-biodegradable.

Small sharp scissors

You will need these to cut around the water-soluble paper, trim wool tops or separate curls.

Wire cutters and pliers

Small wire cutters will be sufficient in order to cut pipe cleaner or other quite thin gauge wire. You may need the pliers to bend the wire if you are unable to use your fingers.

Sewing needle

You will be sewing eyes/mouths onto the fairies, or to put a thread through the top of their head or sew on small details.

Pencil

This will be needed to trace the wing shapes for the Butterfly and Moth Fairy (page 121) onto water-soluble paper.

For lots of extra techniques on how to make fairies in support of the projects here in the book as well as others please visit The Makerss YouTube channel and find The Makerss 'How To...' Fairy tutorial videos in the playlist.

Skills and Techniques

Needle felting

If you have never needle felted before, rest assured that it is one of the easiest crafts to learn. Hold the needle in one hand – between your thumb, index and middle finger – from the top, you will need to stab the needle in and out of wool. Stabbing the needle into wool reduces its size and firms it up. You can sculpt with the needle, attain shapes and add features. The only rule to adhere to is that you go in and out in the same straight line. The movement does not come from your wrist but from your elbow and shoulder. It really is simply described as stabbing a needle into the wool and often going all the way through to the felting mat underneath. You should hear and feel a crunch, caused by the indentations at the working tip of the needle as they catch the fibres on the way in to tangle them up. Pulling the needle out is without obstructions and should feel smooth.

The general rule is that the coarser the fibre the thicker the needle required, the finer, the finer the fibre the needle. You will soon find out if the needle size is suitable for your chosen fibre: if the needle bounces off, or you have to force it into the project you will need to go down a needle size. If you stab the needle and it goes in easily without much happening you are likely to have to go up a size in needle. As the shape gets firmer (the needle will begin to bounce) you may have to go down a needle size too.

Be careful of the needle and try not to stab your fingers. Make sure you keep the needles safe whilst not in use: store them away from children! I recommend using your own needles and do not share. If a needle breaks, make sure you find all parts (usually two to three pieces) and dispose of them safely (such as a sharps bin or wrapping securely).

Most of all enjoy the process of needle felting. It is a magical craft and can be quite addictive.

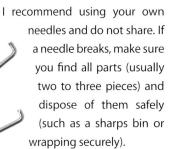

Wrapping

Many of the projects in the book require you to wrap wool around wire. Whether you use wool batts or tops, the important rules are:

1. Keep the wool thin and wispy. For batts split a thin strand off the main batt and tease a little apart, if need be, to make it thinner. You can usually see which way the fibres run, so make sure to split the wool running along the fibres rather than across. For wool tops split a strand off along the main direction of the fibres. To make it thinner either split a thinner part off or pull the fibres gently lengthwise without pulling it apart.
2. Keep the wool flat like a ribbon. Imagine you are wrapping a ribbon and you would therefore not want it to get twisted.
3. Make sure the wool is pulled tight around the wire with every wrap. You can do this best by working close to the wire.

When using florist tape to wrap around the wire, you will have to stretch the florist tape, which will make it sticky and pliable. Rules 2 and 3 (above) apply when wrapping with this tape .

Other useful tips

- Prepare the wire with florist tape, glue or wax to make the wire a little sticky so the fibres do not slip around.
- Use covered wire (paper, cotton) or a 'roughed up' wire. Use serrated wire or run your wire cutter along the length to make scratches on it.
- Once you have established the first wool wraps, turn

the project round and twist the wire instead of folding the wool around the wire each time. Feed the wool through your fingers as you twist the wire.

- When adding more wrap-layers make sure you always wrap the wool around in the same direction so as not to unwrap layers underneath.
- Wrap the last wispy ends of the wool as tight as you can to secure.
- If you have to felt down wispy fibres that have come loose, use a fine needle to stab along the wire rather than into it.

Making curls

Making curls from straight tops: If you are planning on making curls for fairies or gnomes you can use any straight fibres including animal or plant fibres. There are two methods.

1: Crochet

Take a thin strand (0.5–1cm [3/16–3/8in] thick) of the top and crochet into a chain using a 3–3.5mm (C/2–E/4) crochet hook. Try and use as long a strand as you can manage. When you get to the end take the hook out but leave the last loop open (you will have to unravel the chain from there later). Then make the chain soaking wet. Squeeze excess water out gently and leave to dry. You can speed up the process by putting it into a fan oven on a low setting or rest on a radiator or other safe source of heat. Once the strand is completely dry unravel from the top. You will now have a curly strand of wool or other fibre.

2: Skewer or knitting needle

Take a thin strand (0.5–1cm [3/16–3/8in] thick) of the top and wind around a thin skewer (metal, bamboo or wood) or a knitting needle (2.5–3mm [US1–2]). Unlike wrapping the wool flat around the wire, here you allow the wool to twist as you are winding it around the skewer or needle. Be sure you twist the last wispy ends tightly around the wool covered stick to secure them. Then soak it in water and leave to dry. You can speed up the process by putting it into a fan oven on a low setting or rest on a radiator or other safe source of heat. Once the fibre is completely dry

unravel from the skewer or knitting needle. You will now have a strand of locks that resembles corkscrew curls.

Mixing wool

Change the colour of your fibres easily with your fingers. You can also mix wool with silk, curls and plant-based fibres, such as ramie.

Small batches (1–5g [1/32–3/16oz])

Lay the wool batts or tops you wish to mix flat on top of each other and, using both hands, tear these apart between your thumb and index fingers. Lay the strips of wool on top of each other again and repeat. The more you repeat this process the more of a single new colour you will achieve. The less you do it the more mottled and uneven the mixed wool will be.

The principle of mixing colours is the same as mixing paint, i.e. yellow + red = orange

To mix larger quantities use carders or wire dog brushes. Lay the different colour wools you would like to mix flat onto the brush and then brush it with the other brush so that the teeth go in opposite directions. Repeat this process and you may have to 'peel' off the wool in its entirety and repeat the brushing process until the wool is mixed to the desired effect.

A drum carder is useful for larger quantities. These machines work on the same principle as the carders or brushes. A small carder allows you to make one batch (maximum 40g [1½oz]) and I have found three rounds (take the batt off and feed through again three times) gives an even mix.

Wet felting

There is only one project in this book where you will wet felt the wings of the fairy (Water Fairy page 141). This technique is explained within the project.

Sewing

Basic sewing or embroidery is used to make eyes and a mouth for the Rainbow Fairy (page 105).

Large Basic Fairy Body

This is the larger basic body shape that is used for lots of the fairies in this book, such as the Violet Fairy (page 53), the Emerald Fairy (page 47) and the Sun Fairy (page 127) to name just a few. These instructions make a head with a smooth skin-toned cover (no face) and arms and upper body.

SKILL LEVEL
Crafty beginner
FINISHED SIZE
12–20cm (4¾ x 8in)
TECHNIQUES USED
Making people with wire;
wrapping wire/pipe cleaners;
shaping

YOU WILL NEED
WOOL
5g (⅙oz) wool tops in your choice of skin colour – we used pink South American Merino tops
5g (⅙oz) standard core/stuffing batts

EXTRAS
Extra strong thread,
30cm (12in) extra strong pipe cleaners:
1 for the hanging figure or 2 for the standing figure with legs

TOOLS
#38 medium felting needle
Pliers
Felting mat (optional)

Take three-quarters of the pink tops – about 20cm (8in) in length and 2.5cm (1in) wide – and hook it onto the top of the pipe cleaner. Twist the pipe cleaner shut so that the pink wool is trapped and secure. It will look like a moustache!

Push the pink wool up out of the way and wrap the top of the pipe cleaner with the cream core wool, just below the pink tops. Make sure to wrap the wool tightly and keep it flat like a ribbon – the wool should stick to itself.

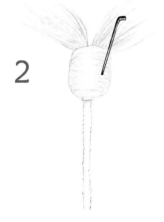

2

3

As the layer of core wool becomes bigger, use your medium needle (#38) to felt it into shape from top to bottom. Do this by holding the shape in your hands but mind your fingers! The finished size should be 3–3.5cm (1¼in–1³/₈in). Push the ball shape up as far as it will go.

Next, fold the pink tops back down and over the round head shape. Make sure that you get a smooth covering, especially where the face will be. There should be no white wool visible, and you may have to spread the pink wool out a little.

Use strong thread to tie the wool below the head. Make sure you have a nice tight cover of wool over the face area (the rest of the head will be covered with hair). If necessary, tie another thread above the first one to make the cover tighter. Don't worry if the bend of the pipe cleaner shows on the top of the head, but make sure it is flat rather than sticking out – just pull at the base of the pipe cleaner.

4

Next, you will need a length of pipe cleaner – see the instructions for the fairy you are making for specific information. If you are making a hanging figure or one with legs, you could cut the body pipe cleaner below the head (leaving enough pipe cleaner to attach the arms to) and use that. For a standing figure, use a new pipe cleaner, which should be at least 15cm (6in) long.

5

Arms

Use the pipe cleaner length to make the arms. Take a wisp of the pink wool and add a thin layer, about 1cm (³/₈in) in length, at the end of the pipe cleaner.

Once you have a thin covering, bend the tip of the pipe cleaner over, making sure that the bend is covered in wool. Then wrap the bend with more pink wool so that it becomes a solid little hand (fist).

6

You can either cover the rest of the arm with the pink wool and your figure will have bare arms, or you can give the figure sleeves. The colour depends on which fairy you are making – see the instructions for that specific project.

7

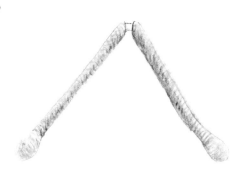

Cover both ends of the pipe cleaner according to your project but leave about 1cm (³/₈in) in the centre uncovered. It pays off to cover the arms neatly with a thin layer.

8

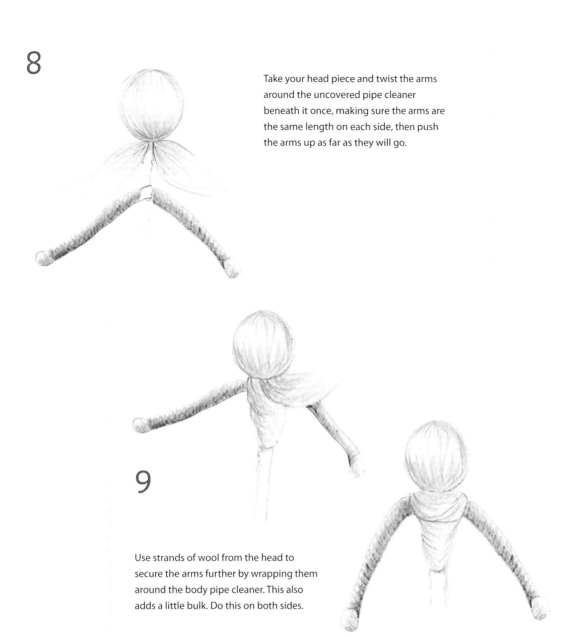

Take your head piece and twist the arms around the uncovered pipe cleaner beneath it once, making sure the arms are the same length on each side, then push the arms up as far as they will go.

9

Use strands of wool from the head to secure the arms further by wrapping them around the body pipe cleaner. This also adds a little bulk. Do this on both sides.

10

You now have the basis of your fairy figure – proceed with the instructions for your project to dress and complete it.

Small Basic Fairy Body

These are the first steps you will need to make the foundation of the smaller figures in this book, such as the Acorn Children (page 71), Wind Sprite (page 117) and the Butterfly and Moth fairies (page 121). You can choose any colour of wool batts to suit your project.

SKILL LEVEL
Crafty beginner
FINISHED SIZE
Up to 10cm (4in)
TECHNIQUES USED
Wire wrapping

YOU WILL NEED
WOOL
1–2g (¹/₂₀oz) wool batts in your choice of skin colour – we used pink Australian Merino batts

2–3g (¹/₉oz) coloured wool batts in your choice of colour for the body – red NZ Merino is used here

EXTRAS
1 x 36cm (14¼in) length of paper-covered wire or flexible steel wire

#22 or #26 gauge

TOOLS
#38 medium felting needle

#40 fine felting needle

#42 extra-fine felting needle

Felting mat

Pliers

PVA glue

1

Cut your length of wire into three equal parts using the pliers. One part will be used for the head and main body, one for arms and one for the legs, if you are making them.

Head

To make the head, take a wispy strand of the pink wool and begin by wrapping it around the end of one wire length. If you find it hard for the wire to 'stick' use a little glue to get started. To add the smallest amount of glue, insert the wire about 2–3cm (¾–1¼in) into the thin nozzle of a glue bottle. Make sure you keep the wool flat and tight, as if you were wrapping a ribbon around wire.

2

Now bend the end of the wire over as close to the end as you can manage – about 0.5cm (⅛in) – use your pliers if you need to. You are trapping the wool in the bend. Wrap the wool over the bend and begin adding bulk. Still keep the wrap tight and flat, teasing the wool as you go. Work close to the wire to stop the wool from tearing. If the wool severs just take a new wisp and continue wrapping as before.

3

Slowly build a rounded shape at the end of the wire. As you build up the wool it may be less willing to just 'stick' to itself. Use your fine needle (#40) to felt wispy ends down. The finished size of the head should be 2cm (¾in). Stab the ball shape all over, especially around the point where the wire sticks out to maintain the ball shape. Use your fine needle (#40) to firm and smooth the head, especially if you are adding eyes and a mouth later.

4

Arms and legs

The arms and legs are both made using the same method. Start out as you did for the head, but this time really make sure you keep the wool thin and wispy when you start wrapping the end of the wire. If you are using glue, use the tiniest amount possible as the hands should be very dainty.

Fold the wire over again as you did before and cover the bend with a thin layer of wool. Then continue wrapping the wire with a thin, tight and flat layer of the wool along the whole length of the wire.

5

Make a hand/foot in the same way at the other end of the wire. Make sure that when you wrap the wool from the other end you are not unwrapping the wool layer underneath. The hands/feet and arms/legs need to look neat. If you are making legs, you will need to wrap the third length of wire as you did for the arms. You should end up with two thinly wrapped wire lengths (arms and legs) and a bare wire with a woollen ball at one end (head and body).

6

Attach the arms by twisting the wire around the bare body wire once. Make sure the arms are the same length. You can push the arms up if they are not already right underneath the head. If you are not making legs then wrap the main body wire with the body wool, bend in half and wrap tightly into a neat, slightly tapered shape of about 4cm (1½in) length and 2cm (¾in) width.

7

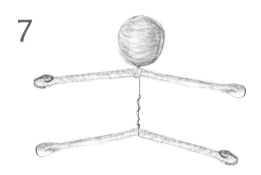

If you have made legs, lay these onto the bare wire about 2cm (¾in) away from the arms and bend the bare body wire around them in the middle. Secure the legs by winding the bare body wire around the middle of the legs a few times, then tidy it away along the body pointing upwards. Cut away any excess. Bend the legs down.

8

Move the arms up out of the way, and then take your coloured wool batts and begin wrapping the body around the middle and between the legs. You can be a little more generous with the wool wrap now as you will need to build up a little bulk. Felt the wool wrap down to make a firm and neat body shape. The body should remain a straight sided shape.

9

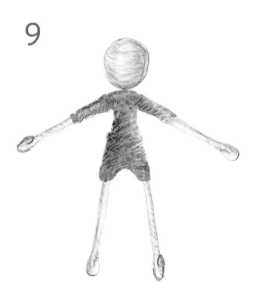

Finally, use wispy strands of the same wool to give the figure short sleeves (like a tight T-shirt) or you could cover the whole arms just leaving the hands exposed. If you wrap the wool tightly and flat, you will not have to felt it down. Your figure is now ready to be personalised.

Earth

Wild Rose Fairy

The wild rose is one of my favourite flowers. It is also the ancestor of all roses that we see today. I love it for its simple beauty, which really needs to be admired in nature and cannot be brought into the house. Wild, beautiful and independent!

SKILL LEVEL
Crafty beginner

FINISHED SIZE
20cm (8in) long

TECHNIQUES USED
Wire wrapping and a little needle felting

To be able to suspend your fairy in the air, use silky thread to hang the fairy up, by going in and out of the top of the finished head with a threaded needle.

YOU WILL NEED

WOOL
5g (1/6oz) standard core batts
3g (1/8oz) pale green NZ Merino batts
6g (1/5oz) pink South American Merino tops
3g (1/8oz) neon pink Australian Merino tops
2g (1/12oz) white extra-fine Merino tops

EXTRAS
3g (1/8oz) yellow Bluefaced Leicester curls
1g (1/24oz) fuchsia pink Angelina fibre
1 x 30cm (12in) extra-strong pipe cleaner
Length of rose lace trim
1 x tiny bird decoration
1m (39½in) extra-strong thread
50cm (19¾in) silky thread

TOOLS
#38 medium felting needle
Sewing needle
PVA clear-drying glue
Pliers
Scissors
An iron
Parchment or greaseproof paper
Pink or purple waterproof pen
Felting mat (optional)
1m (40in) extra-strong thread
Sewing needle
Few strands bouclé yarn in the colour of your choice for hair

FOR THE WILD ROSES
1g (1/24oz) space-dyed berries wool tops (pinks)
Wisp of bleached-white Australian Merino batts or white Cape Merino batts
Wisp of golden-yellow NZ Merino
5 x 20cm (1/8 x 8in) wool-viscose felt in white

1

Make a base shape according to the Large Basic Fairy Body instructions on page 16. In Step 4 (see page 18) use a 16–18cm (6¼–7in) length of pipe cleaner taken from the long body pipe cleaner. Use the pink wool tops to make the arms. Your fairy should now have pink-coloured head, arms and hands.

2

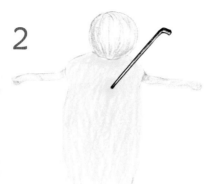

Take the pale-green wool and flatten it into a shape that fits on the palm and fingers of your hand. This piece should not be too thick, so remove some layers if necessary. Make a hole in the centre. Slip the shape over the fairy's head so that the longer sides run down the front and back of the body. Make sure that the side of the head with the smoothest pink cover faces forwards. Felt the upper body cover down gently and slip the arm cover up the upper arm as far as possible.

3

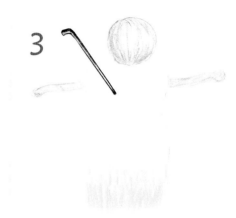

Next, take the white extra-fine Merino top and make a hole in the middle of it. Just as you did with the green wool, place the white tops over the head and felt it gently onto the body. Stab under the arms and above the waist but keep it as unfelted as possible. The neck should be closed and covered in white.

4

Take the neon pink top and split it in half lengthwise. Fold one end in and attach it to the waist at the front, working in a straight line below the white by stabbing along the edge. Repeat the same process on the back and bring the two sides together so that they meet and felt down at the waist only. The sides will remain open to expose a little pale green 'underskirt'.

5

Place one end of your rose lace trim in the centre of the back waist (where the white meets the pink). Wrap it once around the waist tightly, so that the trim meets itself at the back again. Cut the trim between two roses and hold it in place at the back with your finger. Then use a tiny wisp of wool (if you have green or any other colour left) and gently felt down with your felting needle through the trim and into body of the fairy to secure the waistband in place.

6

Hair

Use the messy yellow curls to make the hair. You may have to cut small strands off and even pick some plant material out of them – the idea is that her hair is quite wild! Felt the hair onto the side of the head framing the face. Once the sides of the face are done, cover the rest of the head. You can keep the curls long or short by picking longer curls out and attaching them separately.

7

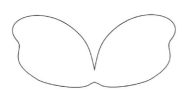

8

Parchment sits on top of template

Wings

First fold your parchment or greaseproof paper in half. Lay one half of your folded paper over the wing template (below) so that you can still see the template through it. You may wish to trace the template onto a blank piece of paper first.

Turn on your iron to allow it to heat up to its maximum setting. Take small wisps of Angelina fibre and lay these on top of the parchment, following the shape of the wing, for example, start at the bottom centre and follow the shape of the wings up towards the tips. Do this on both wings. Gently slide the template away from underneath, then cover the Angelina fibres with the other half of the parchment.

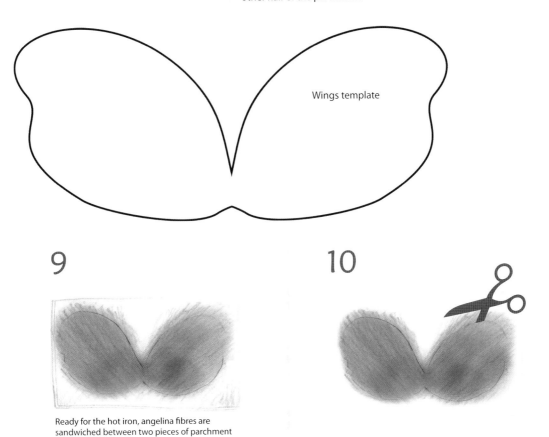

Wings template

9

Ready for the hot iron, angelina fibres are sandwiched between two pieces of parchment

10

Place the hot iron on top of the paper with the Angelina fibres sandwiched between the two halves. Only run the iron across it for five to ten seconds. You will see that the colour of the pink fibres becomes more vibrant.

Open the paper and you will see that the individual Angelina fibres have fused together into a single sheet. Lay the template underneath the sheet and draw the outline of the wings onto the fused fibres with your waterproof pen. Cut out the shape of the wings from the fused Angelina fibres. If your pen matches the colour of the wings, it will not be noticeable, or you can cut inside the line.

11

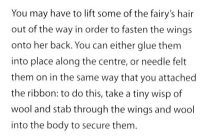

12

You may have to lift some of the fairy's hair out of the way in order to fasten the wings onto her back. You can either glue them into place along the centre, or needle felt them on in the same way that you attached the ribbon: to do this, take a tiny wisp of wool and stab through the wings and wool into the body to secure them.

Finally, cut some individual roses from the remaining lace trim to decorate your fairy to your liking. Glue or sew the roses on. You can 'freshen up' the look of the dress by teasing fibres out at the base – take care not to make the dress too short or damage the fairy as you do this.

Making the Wild Roses

Size: 8 x 8cm (3¹/₈in)

Use a scrap of parchment paper to trace the petal template below, which is actual size.
Cut out and use as the pattern piece for your flowers.

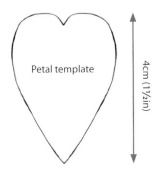

Petal template

4cm (1½in)

These flowers look lovely when in a group

1

Cut five petal shapes out of the felt piece using the template. Take the pink wool top which has a range of bright coloured pink tones and tear off a small wisp and lay onto one petal shape. Felt down with your medium needle but leave a tiny white edge as small as you can manage. The colours will slightly vary as you take different parts of the top.

2

Lay them out so that the pointy ends meet and add a wisp of white wool into the centre. Felt on top of the ends of the petals making sure that they get held together in that way. You may have to stab into the tip of the petal at a shallow angle towards the centre to stop the petal moving outward

3

Check that each petal is secured before adding a tiny amount of the golden yellow on top of the white. Felt down. The petals should bend upwards slightly, which gives it a more natural look too. Then take a tiny wisp of the pink top and add five dots into the centre onto the yellow wool to give the impression of flower stamen.

Amethyst Fairy

Amethyst is the birthstone for February, and it stands for grounding, tranquillity and calm. Another stunning product of nature.

SKILL LEVEL
Crafty beginner

FINISHED SIZE
18cm (7in) long

TECHNIQUES USED
Wire wrapping and a little needle felting

YOU WILL NEED

WOOL
5g (1/6oz) cream, standard core batts
4g (1/7oz) light purple NZ Merino batts
2g (1/12oz) dark purple NZ Merino batts
6g (1/5oz) pale brown or beige dyed Australian Merino tops
5g (1/6oz) purple-tones Australian Merino tops
3g (1/8oz) short, purple Bluefaced Leicester curls

EXTRAS
2 x 30cm (12in) extra-strong pipe cleaners
25 x 15cm (10 x 6in) piece of purple tulle with sparkly dots
1 x amethyst stone
1g (1/24oz) of mixed purple beads
1g (1/24oz) of purple-pink Angelina fibre
10cm (4in) length of purple sequin trim
1m (39½in) extra-strong thread
50cm (19¾in) silky thread

TOOLS
#38 medium felting needle
Sewing needle
PVA glue
Pliers
Scissors
An iron
Parchment or greaseproof paper
Pink or purple waterproof pen
Felting mat (optional)
Thin sewing needle (to fit beads)

1

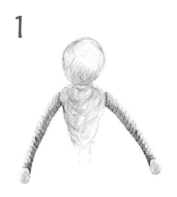

Make a basic fairy shape by following the Large Basic Fairy Body instructions on page 16. In Step 4 (see page 18) you should use a 16–18cm (6¼–7in) length of pipe cleaner, so use the second pipe cleaner to cut to size. Use the pale brown wool tops to make the hands, face and body and the dark-purple wool batts to thinly cover the arms. When wrapping the arms, you will have to work very close to the pipe cleaner as the wool batts have shorter fibres.

2

Next take some dark purple batts and a tiny wisp of the purple-pink Angelina fibre and mix them thoroughly. (See 'Mixing wool' on page 15 for how to mix wool colours together).

Keep the fibres running in the same direction if you can. Apply a thin layer of the mix over the top of both arms. As before, keep the layer thin and tight and work close to the wire.

3

Legs

To make the legs, take 15cm (6in) of pipe cleaner and, as you did for the arms, cover the ends of it with pale brown tops, so that 1.5cm (½in) of foot is covered. Then mix some more dark purple and Angelina fibre and cover the legs all the way from one foot to the other. Bend each foot in by about 1cm (³∕₈in).

4

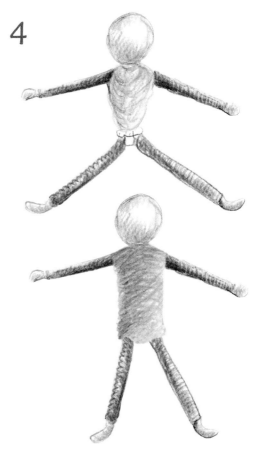

Now fasten the legs in place by twisting the body pipe cleaner around the centre of the legs. Take the light purple wool and wrap thin layers around the fairy's legs to secure them further. Then thinly cover the rest of the upper body with this same lighter colour.

5

Dress

Take a pinch of light purple wool and flatten it into a shape about 15 x 10cm (6 x 4in) in size. Make a hole in the centre. Fit this over the head of the fairy so that the longer sides are running down the front and back.

Push up her arms to hold the wool cover in place then use your needle to felt it down on her upper body and around her arms.

6

Shorten the purple dress to expose the feet and lower legs by gently tearing off wisps of wool at the bottom. This is also a useful way to tidy up the hem of the dress.

7

Next take the long piece of multi-shaded purple-tones tops and make a hole in the centre as you did before. Slip this over the fairy's head. Again, use the arms to keep the tops in place and tease the fibres so that they make a cover all around the fairy.

8

Take the tulle and fold it into a long, thin strip (about 1cm [³/₈in] wide), ensuring the sparkly dots are on the outside. Tie it around the fairy's waist, just beneath the arms. Pull it tight and secure it by felting a tiny wisp of light purple wool over the tie.

The ends of the Tulle fabric can be spread out to hang down the front of the fairy. Make sure that the wool on the arms looks the same on each side and spread out the tulle over the dress if you like.

9

Hair

The purple curls for the hair are hand dyed and they sometimes get slightly felted together during the dyeing process. To separate them, use small, pointed scissors to cut them apart along the line of the curls as well as you can. Once you have sorted through the curls so that you have manageable batches and have checked that they are running in the right direction, it's time to felt them onto the fairy's head.

10

Take a small batch and felt them onto one side of the face first. To cover more of the head, tease the curls out widthways with your fingers – this also makes it easier to felt them down.

Next, cover the other side so that the whole face is framed, then fill in the back of the head. If you have any curls left add more where they're needed.

11

Take the sequin trim and place it around the top part of the fairy's head. Thread your sparkly thread onto a sewing needle and sew the headband closed at the back of the head. Using the same needle and thread (and checking that the needle fits some of the smallest beads) sew the little glass beads all over the head.

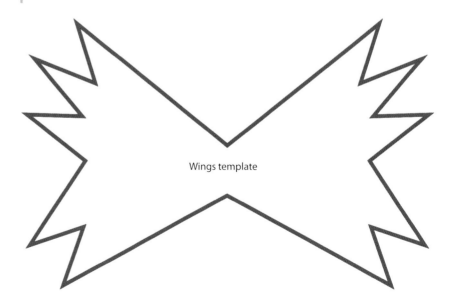

Wings template

12

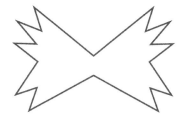

Wings

First fold your parchment/greaseproof paper in half, then open it out again. Lay one half of your folded parchment or greaseproof paper over the wing template on page 36 so that you can still see the template through it. (You may wish to trace the template onto a blank piece of paper first.)

13

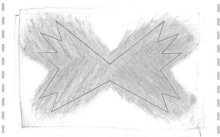

Take small wisps of purple-pink Angelina fibre and lay these on top of the parchment, following the shape of the wing. Do this on both sides of the wings. Turn on your iron to allow it to heat up to its maximum setting. Gently slide the template away from underneath the parchment/greaseproof paper and then cover the Angelina fibres with the other half of the parchment.

14

Place the hot iron on top of the paper with the Angelina fibre sandwiched between the two halves. Only run the iron across it for five to ten seconds. You will see that the colour of the Angelina fibres becomes more vibrant.

15

Open the parchment/greaseproof paper and your individual Angelina fibres will now have fused into a solid sheet. Lay the template underneath the sheet (it will still be see-through) as you did before ironing. Using your waterproof pen, draw the outline of the wings onto the fused fibres. and then carefully cut out the shape.

16

Use any wisps of purple wool you have left to felt the wings into place by laying the wool on the centre of them and then stabbing into the fairy's back. Alternatively, you can attach the wings with a dab of glue.

You may want to give the amethyst quartz crystal a rinse with water to remove any natural dust. Once it's clean and dry, place it in your fairy's arms.

Daisy Fairy

The daisy flower in Norse Mythology is Freya's sacred flower. Freya is the goddess of love, beauty and fertility and the daisy is the symbol of new beginnings.

SKILL LEVEL
Crafty beginner
FINISHED SIZE
18cm (7in) long
TECHNIQUES USED
Wire wrapping and a little needle felting

YOU WILL NEED
WOOL BATTS
7g (¼oz) cream standard core/stuffing
4g ((¹⁄₇oz) golden-yellow NZ Merino
1g (¹⁄₂₄oz) light-yellow NZ Merino
1g (¹⁄₂₄oz) green rainbow drops NZ Merino
5g (¹⁄₆oz) strawberry-blonde straight mohair yarn

WOOL TOPS
5g (¹⁄₆oz) pink-dyed South American Merino
5g (¹⁄₆oz) white extra-fine Australian Merino

EXTRAS
2 x 30cm (12in) extra strong pipe cleaners
18 x 10cm (7 x 4in) piece of daisy tulle fabric
1.5m (59in) extra strong thread
1m (39½in) silky thread
2 x silk daisies

TOOLS
#38 medium felting needle
Sewing needle
PVA glue
Pliers
Scissors
Felting mat (optional)

FOR THE DAISIES (MAKES 8)
WOOL BATTS
5g (¹⁄₆oz) bleached white Australian Merino
7g (¼oz) golden-yellow NZ Merino
1g (¹⁄₂₄oz) hot-pink NZ Merino
4g (¹⁄₇oz) lichen-green Mountain sheep

EXTRAS
20 x 20cm (8 x 8in) piece water-soluble paper
60cm (24in) satin leaf ribbon

TOOLS
Felting needles (#38 medium, #40 fine)
Felting mat
Small bowl of warm water
Kitchen paper or tea towel

1

Make a base shape according to the Large Basic Fairy Body instructions on page 16. In Step 4 (see page 18) you should use a 16–18cm (6¼–7in) length of pipe cleaner, so use the second pipe cleaner and cut it to length. Use the pink wool to make the hands and the light-yellow wool batts to cover the arms thinly. If you prefer, you can also use the golden-yellow or green rainbow wool batts – it's your choice. The head should be about 5cm (2in) in diameter. If your head is a little smaller or larger that's fine!

2

Legs

Take a 15cm (6in) length of pipe cleaner cut from the main body pipe cleaner and cover the ends in pink wool tops, as you did for the hands. Cover the remainder of the pipe cleaner with the green rainbow wool batts. Make sure you keep the cover thin and tight.

Bend the leg pipe cleaner in the middle and wrap the main body pipe cleaner around the bend to secure the legs. The body, from the base of the head to the top of the centre bend of the legs, should measure no more than 4–5cm (1½–2in).

3

Take the golden yellow wool batts and, using your hands, shape them into a flat sheet, measuring roughly 13cm (5in) wide by 15cm (6in) long. Make sure it is a continuous flat sheet. Make a hole in the centre for the fairy's head to fit through and slip the head through the hole so that the

longer parts of the sheet hang down equal lengths at the front and the back. Push the arms up and felt the yellow wool down away from the upper arms. Felt the upper body down slightly. It works best to felt into the wool gently and at a shallow angle.

4

Tuck the ends of the yellow fibres neatly up into the gap between the fairy and the yellow dress, so that from underneath it looks like a golden ring – this will become part of the hidden flower visible only when you turn the fairy upside down.

Take the soft, white wool tops and split into half so that you have two similar length strands of 10–15cm (4–6in) each. Lay the fairy onto one half and then lay the second half over the top of your fairy. Next, take your remaining extra-strong thread and tie it around the fairy's waist tightly. Secure with a knot.

6

Gently pull the top-half ends of the white wool strands down. You may have to redistribute the skirt so that the sides are closed. Do this by gently pulling the tops along sideways and spreading them out.

Secure the top of the skirt – and at the same time expose more of the golden-yellow upper body – by stabbing into the tied waist with your felting needle. We will come back to the skirt later.

7

Hair

Using the strawberry-blonde mohair yarn, make looped strands of about 10cm (4in) long (do not cut the ends yet). You can probably work with six loops at a time. Felt the top of the mohair loops onto the top of the fairy's head. Start by framing the face. Leave the ends of the yarn hanging down at the side but make sure that the yarn is felted onto the head securely. Do the same on the other side of the face.

8

Then fill in the back of the head in the same way, always working with the same length loops and spreading the yarn strands out to cover the head so that no pink is visible.

9

Now use much shorter loops (3–4cm [1¼–1½in]) to felt a fringe onto your fairy. Once this is done, take your scissors and cut the looped strands open at the bottom to form the fringe. Trim the fairy's hair to even out the length if you wish and/or add more strands of wool to give a fuller head of hair.

10

Twist the ends of the skirt into petal shapes – the more petals you manage to make the better, because daisies have lots of them. Use your scissors to cut the ends off the petals so that the legs are visible, then twist the straight ends back into pointy ends.

Each petal will now be shorter and neater.

11

Wings

Use the scissors to round off the corners of the daisy tulle fabric. Use extra-strong thread (or a thin strand of white wool) to tie the centre of the tulle together so that it forms a bow. Use a little of the white tops (you could use the off cuts from the skirt) and felt the wings onto the fairy by laying the wool into the centre of the wing and felting down into the upper body.

12

If you turn the fairy upside down you should be able to see a whole flower, with white petals, a yellow centre and the legs could look like flower stamen. You can neaten up the yellow centre with your needle if needed. It is not too late to make more petals by splitting the existing ones into half for a fuller skirt.

13

You can push the stems of the silk daisies through the loop of pipe cleaners in the fairy's hand for her to hold them securely. Or why not make a daisy chain to accompany your fairy?

Making the Daisies

1

Cut your water-soluble paper into 16 equal squares, each 5 x 5cm (2 x 2in). Take two squares and round the edges into a circular shape. You need two circles per daisy.

2

Take a wisp of the bleached-white wool and felt flat onto the water-soluble paper disc. Lift off regularly to prevent it fastening to your mat. Felt only from one side. In any case the wool can spill out over the edge of the paper. Make sure that the disc is filled evenly with no gaps.

3

Take a tiny amount of pink and a little more of the white and mix the two fibres into a softer pink and felt a tiny amount (a dusting) only into the centre of the white disc.

4

Next take a little golden-yellow and roll into a ball between your fingers. Add to the centre and felt down around the edges first so the ball shape remains. Next, felt the centre. Make another disc with the other water-soluble paper the same but do not add the yellow this time.

5

Have a bowl of warm water at the ready and dip both shapes into it only quickly. The aim is to dissolve the water-soluble paper but not to rinse all the residue out, as this will help to solidify the shape once dry. Squeeze excess water out, which often helps to dissolve the paper and leave to dry. For speed place onto a radiator or similar source of gentle heat.

6

Once dry the shapes should feel stiff. Use your scissors and cut around the shape neatening the edges. Use the scissors and cut the petals, from the outer edge towards the centre stopping at the yellow middle, about 20 times. Cut both discs, making sure that the cuts on the disc without the yellow centre are no longer than 1cm (³/₈in).

7

Place the two shapes on top of each other so the one with the yellow middle is on top and stab your needle into the yellow to felt the two together. Add more yellow wool to build a yellow domed centre. Make sure to also stab deeply around the yellow which will the petals to come up and give the daisy a nice shape.

Make 7 more daisies.

8

Take your first daisy and turn it over, so the back of it is facing up. With the right side of the green ribbon facing down, lay the ribbon onto the daisy, positioning the flower between two pairs of leaves. Using your medium or fine needle, felt wisps of green wool over the top of the ribbon and into the back of the daisy. Stab gently and carefully as you felt into the ribbon and ensure that the green wool does not come out at the other side.

Attach all your daisies onto the ribbon in the same way. Your daisy chain is finished! Why not try making other kinds of flowers in a similar way? Have fun being creative!

Emerald Fairy

Nature does not disappoint with this stunning
green precious stone. Emerald is the birthstone
for May and stands for Spring.

YOU WILL NEED

WOOL

6g (¹/₅oz) green shimmer NZ Merino batts,

8g (²/₇oz) dark-brown Milk sheep batts,

6g (¹/₅oz) green-tones Australian Merino tops,

3g (¹/₈oz) black Little Loopy Locks yarn

EXTRAS

2 x 30cm (12in) extra-strong pipe cleaners

1m (39½in) brown embroidery thread

50cm (19¾in) silky thread.

1 x dark-green stone,

10 x light-green rhinestones

2 x green feathers

10cm (4in) of green/blue sequin trim (optional)

TOOLS

#38 medium felting needle

Sewing needle

PVA glue

Scissors

Felting mat (optional)

SKILL LEVEL
Crafty beginner

FINISHED SIZE
22cm (8¾in) tall

TECHNIQUES USED
Wire wrapping and a
little needle felting

1

Make a basic fairy shape by following the Large Basic Fairy Body instructions on page 16. Use dark brown Milk sheep batts to make and cover the head of the fairy. For the arms, use a 16–18cm (6¼–7in) length of pipe cleaner taken from the long body pipe cleaner. Use the dark-brown batts to wrap the hands and the shimmer-green batts to thinly cover the arms. Carefully separate thin strips of shimmer green from the side of the batts – rather than tearing the whole piece apart – as you will need an intact wad for later.

2

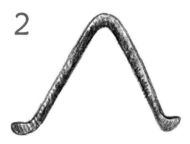

Legs

Next, take the entire second pipe cleaner and cover it thinly with the dark-brown wool. The finished size from toe to toe should be about 25cm (10in). Bend each end in by about 2cm (¾in) to form the feet.

3

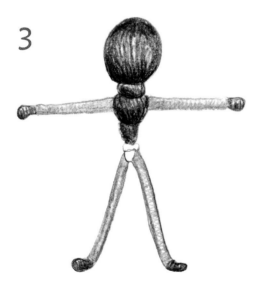

Use the green shimmer wool to wrap the legs, leaving both feet and about 2–3cm (¾–1¼in) of leg uncovered at the bend between the legs. Continue to wrap with shimmer green until the legs are about 8mm (¼in) thick. Attach the legs to the body by wrapping the main body pipe cleaner length around the bend. The top of the legs should be as far from the head as the head is wide – about 4cm (1½in).

4

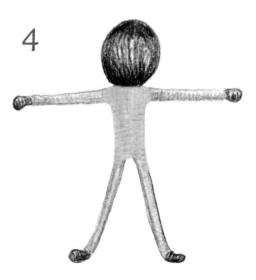

Use more of the green shimmer wool to wrap the lower body and between the legs to further secure them. Felt the fibres down to fasten them on by stabbing your needle into the wool along the pipe cleaner.

5

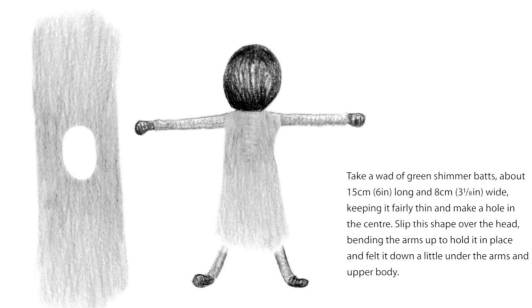

Take a wad of green shimmer batts, about 15cm (6in) long and 8cm (3⅛in) wide, keeping it fairly thin and make a hole in the centre. Slip this shape over the head, bending the arms up to hold it in place and felt it down a little under the arms and upper body.

6

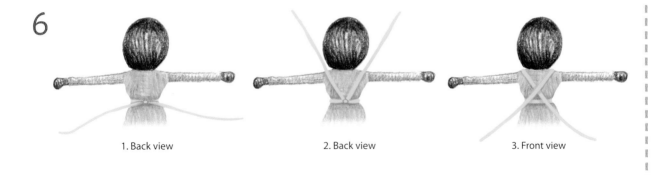

1. Back view

2. Back view

3. Front view

4. Back view

5. Front view

Next, separate a thin strand of the lightest green from the green tops, about 30cm (12in) long. Lay the strand across the front of the fairy, just under the arms. Turn your fairy over so that the back is facing up and tie the strand tightly, then secure it with a knot at the back (see 1. above).

With the back of the fairy still facing, lay the two strands of green tops over the shoulders (see 2. above). Turn your fairy over and cross the strands over at the front, then take them down towards the waist again (see 3. above).

Turn your fairy over once more, so her back is facing up and secure the two strands coming around the waist with a knot (see 4. above). Turn your fairy over to the front and see the crossed-over straps (see 5. above).

7

When you turn the fairy face up again, work a little more on felting the shoulders and to shape the upper body, especially if the two sides are a slightly different size.

8

Take your green-tones tops and split them in half by holding on to the ends and gently pulling them apart, allowing the fibres to slither away from each other in the middle.

You should now have two shorter lengths. Now split off a thin strand of wool, just as you did for the waist tie – this will be hidden later so the shade of green you use is not important.

9

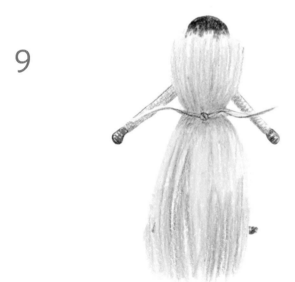

Lay your fairy on top of one half of the green tops, then lay the other half on top of the fairy. You should have one third of the length positioned above the waist and two thirds below. Spread out the fibres sideways as best as you can without messing them up.

Take the thin strand of wool and tie it around the fairy's middle, making sure it sits below the waist tie you made earlier. Pull it tight and secure with a knot.

10

Gently pull the fibres that are above the tie down and stroke them so that they will stay in place. This layer of tops will be shorter than the layer underneath.

11

Hair

Take the little loopy locks and wind lengths of about 8cm (3¹/₈in) around your fingers eight or nine times, then cut the end of the yarn. Needle felt the loops of one end onto the top of the fairy's head, so it frames one side of the face. Felt along the head but leave the other end of the loops hanging down. Repeat this for the other side too and for the back of the head. Three portions of the loops should be enough to cover the whole head and frame the face. Add more if needed but you may have yarn left over at the end.

12

Optional: Take the length of the sequin trim and place it around the top part of the head. You can add a little hair wool at the back and felt onto the ends to secure it or sew the trim closed.

13

To form the wings, position the two feathers on the fairy's back by placing them into the crossed strands of wool.
Use a tiny wisp of green shimmer batts to felt over the centre of the wings so that they are fastened securely on.

14

Add the little rhinestones to the fairy's dress with clear-drying glue. You can keep the green tops of the fairy's dress long and just tidy them by tearing wisps off, or you could cut them shorter and twist the ends between your fingers to make them pointy.

Violet Fairy

I love this modest little flower that, when you look closely, is one of the most beautiful flowers around. Pansies are also a member of the same family of plants.

YOU WILL NEED

WOOL

Dyed South American Merino tops:

   5g (⅙oz) pink – 20cm (8in) long, double-finger width

   7g (¼oz) purple – 40cm (15¾in) long

   1g (¹⁄₂₄oz) black – 20cm (8in) long, 1cm (³⁄₈in) width

1g (¹⁄₂₄oz) berries space-dyed Australian Merino Tops – 20cm (8in) long, 1cm (³⁄₈in) width

5g (⅙oz) standard core batts

5g (⅙oz) light-yellow New Zealand Merino batts

EXTRAS

10 x 12cm (4 x 4¾in) off-white felt sheet

1 x 30cm (12in) extra-strong pipe cleaner

1m (39½in) extra-strong thread

Crystal gemstones

TOOLS

#38 medium felting needle

Sewing needle

PVA glue

Felt-tipped pens in yellow, purple and pink

Pliers

Scissors

Felting mat (optional)

SKILL LEVEL
Crafty beginner

FINISHED SIZE
20cm (8in) long

TECHNIQUES USED
Wire wrapping and a little needle felting

1

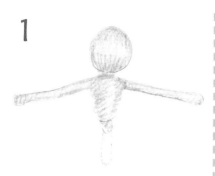

Make a base shape according to the Large Basic Fairy Body instructions on page 16. In Step 4 (see page 18) you should use a 16–18cm (6¼–7in) length of pipe cleaner. Use the pink wool tops to make the arms. Before you start using the other colours of wool, put aside the tiniest of wisps of the yellow, purple and black.

2

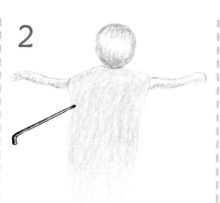

Take the light-yellow wool batts and flatten them out to about the width of your hand, making sure the fibres run lengthways. Make a hole in the centre. Slip the fairy's head through the hole. This layer will add bulk to the figure and acts as a base layer. Pinch the sides in underneath the arms and gently stab with your needle. You will be felting the chest and tummy part only, so that the upper arms are freed up and the upper body is a little firmer. You can do this by holding the fairy in your hand. Mind your fingers!

3

Next, take the purple wool top and make a hole in the centre. Slip this over the fairy, then take the strand of 'berries' pink and purple tops and get ready to tie it around the waist, right below the arms. Make sure you tie it tightly and neatly so that the upper arms of the fairy are the same on both sides and remain slightly puffy. Do not worry if the top layer is much longer than the base layer or slightly uneven.

4

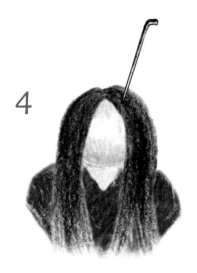

Hair

You can keep the fairy's hair, made from the black wool tops, straight or make your own curls (see p15). Start by using short strands to fasten the hair to the side of the head. Felt these down with your needle to create a frame around the face, then cover the back of the head. You will need to tease any homemade curls apart a little to add volume and cover. Your Violet Flower Fairy will look lovely with or without curls!

5

To finish, add little glue dots onto the dress to attach sparkly crystal gemstones for decoration, or you might prefer to stick on some little violet flowers (see the next page) you have made.

Making the Violets

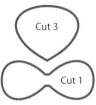
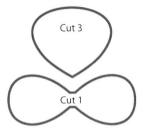
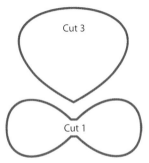

Petal templates for 3 sizes of flower

1

Using the templates (right), choose which size violet you want to make and for each flower cut (from your sheet of white felt) three identical large petals and one that looks like a figure 8. You can colour your pansies with wool by stabbing it onto the petals; however, because the flowers are so small this can be tricky, so it is easier to colour them in using felt-tipped pens.

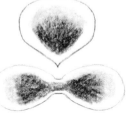

Start by using yellow to colour one large petal and the figure 8 petal. Leave white edges. Then add purple on top just leaving a little yellow edge.

Colour the two large petals, first with pink or a lighter purple (leaving an edge) and add darker purple towards the pointy end, over the top, leaving a white border as before.

2

Lay the petals out as pictured right:
1. One large petal almost covers the other identical large petal.
2. The figure 8 overlaps the tips of the two large ones.
3. The last large petal reaches into the centre of the figure 8.

Use a tiny wisp of black (or purple and black mix) and felt into the centre to fasten all the petals together. Allow some of the dark wool to spill into the three petals with the yellow.

Finally, felt an even tinier yellow spot in the middle of the black or purple black mix.

3

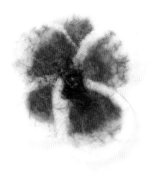

Decorate your fairy to your liking with the little violets: put them in her hair, on her dress, have her holding a flower. You can glue them on if necessary. How tiny can you make your violets?

Wood Mouse

Sometimes known as a long-tailed field mouse, they make their homes in woods and rough grassland. I love this little mouse for its rich reddish coat and large ears and eyes.

SKILL LEVEL
Crafty beginner to advanced
FINISHED SIZE
8–9cm (3⅛–3½in)
TECHNIQUES USED
Wrapping wool
around wire

YOU WILL NEED
WOOL BATTS
8g (²/₇oz) grey-brown Country sheep
1g (¹/₂₄oz) brown Mountain sheep
1g (¹/₂₄oz) fox-rust brown NZ Merino
1g (¹/₂₄oz) pink NZ Merino
Wisp of cream luxury organic core wool

EXTRAS
1 x 36cm (14in) length of #26 gauge
paper-covered wire
10 x 4cm (1½in) long cream horsetail hairs
2 x 5mm black glue-in eye

TOOLS
#36 coarse felting needle
#38 medium felting needle
#40 fine felting needle
Scissors
PVA glue (clear drying)
Wire cutters or old scissors to cut wire

1

Nose and tail

Take your 36cm (14in) length of wire and cut two 10cm (4in) lengths off, which will leave you with a length of 16cm (6¼in). Dip the end – about 2cm (¾in) – into the glue to cover it with a tiny amount. Then take your pink wool and wrap the glue-covered end with a thin, flat layer of wool.

2

Bend the end of the wire in by 0.5cm (⅛in) and wrap the bent end with more wool, so it measures about 0.5cm (⅛in) in width and secure the wool a little along the wire. You have made the mouse's nose. Remember this technique because you will use it for the feet too. You can use your fine needle to felt the wrapped end down but mind the wire!

3

Dip the opposite end of the wire into the glue and repeat the same process to make a tiny tail tip using the grey-brown wool. Continue wrapping the same wool all the way along the wire to the nose. If you have Vaseline or similar you can add a little to your fingers and wrap the wool so that the grease makes the wool smoother as you wrap it – this is especially important for the tail end, which needs to appear less fluffy.

4

Legs

Take one of the two 10cm wires and, using the technique described in Steps 1 and 2, wrap each end with a pink foot about 1cm (³/₈in) long. Then add the grey-brown wool and wrap along from the foot for about 3cm (1¼in). Repeat on the other side. Use the remaining wire to make the second set of legs in the same way.

5

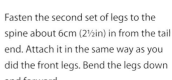

Take one set of the legs and a strand of the grey-brown wool. Lay the centre of the legs along the body wire about 4cm (1½in) away from the nose. Secure the legs to the body wire with the grey-brown wool by winding it around the cross join.

Fasten the second set of legs to the spine about 6cm (2½in) in from the tail end. Attach it in the same way as you did the front legs. Bend the legs down and forward.

6

Head and body

Now it is time to build up the head and body. Start by wrapping layers of the grey-brown wool around the head making sure that the head is bulkier at the top and tapers towards the nose. Felt the wool down using your medium or coarse needle as you add layers.

Use the template (below) to check the size of the head and do the same when you are making the body. Make sure you keep the mouse in the finished pose a much as possible so that you can see where bulk needs adding.

7

As you get closer to the finished size you will need to stop wrapping the wool and instead add small wads or patches to build up bulk in a more targeted way, for example, around the tummy and bottom. Felt the wool wads down, making sure to cover more of the legs because they are pulled up under the body and in the end only the feet will show.

8

Keep adding wads where needed (check against the template). You will find that you may have to revisit some areas as you add bulk and work on other parts. Once the mouse fits the template you will be covering it with the final coat and adding features such as ears and eyes.

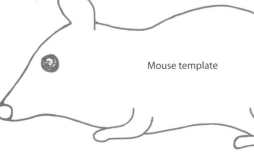

Mouse template

9

Ears

Take a small pinch of the brown Mountain sheep batts and felt it flat on your mat, making a semicircle of about 1.5cm (⁵/₈in). Tuck in any wispy fibres that fall outside the circular line to make a neat edge. Leave the open part at the bottom of the semicircle unfelted. These fibres are great to hold onto while shaping the ear and will become the base that gets felted onto the head. Felt from both sides and add a little pink on one side at the end. Make two ears in this way.

10

Spread the wispy ends of the ears out over the head and felt them down slightly to the sides of the head, facing forwards, about 3cm (1¼in) away from the tip of the nose. You can manipulate their position and size by changing where and how you stab your needle.

If you need to reduce the size use a coarse needle and felt along the ear at a shallow angle into the head. Make the ears face forward and make them slightly hollow by stabbing right into the earhole.

11

Top coat fur

From now on you will be working on the topcoat using a new wool mix of mostly brown Mountain sheep with a little less fox-rust brown. Mix small batches – just as much as you can work between your fingers. When mixing the wool, lay the fibres down and tease them apart, always teasing in the same direction.

Take a wisp of the new mix and lay it onto the face/head in front of the ears. When applying the topcoat, always lay the fibres in the direction that the fur would naturally go. Felt the topcoat down.

12

Now start laying the mix down on the rest of the mouse, starting on the bottom and working your way forwards – cover the mouse's sides as you go. Once the mouse is covered add a couple of lines to emphasise some of the shapes, such as the haunches and shoulders. Also stab between shoulder blades.

13

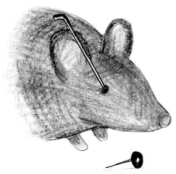

Eyes

Use your felting needle to make a hole in the side of the head halfway between the nose and the ear. Insert your needle all the way to the fatter part of the head. Be mindful of where the needle comes out. Take the needle out and put the pin of the glue-in eye into the hole. Repeat on the other side of the head. If the eyes are in line add a dab of glue behind them without taking them out altogether and push them back in – leave them to dry.

14

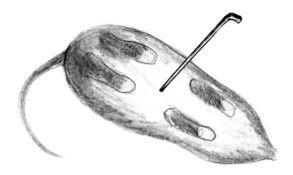

Tummy

Turn your mouse upside down. Add tiny wisps of the cream wool to the tummy and underneath the head. Remember you have wire inside the whole shape so you can shape the mouse a little, by lifting the nose up off the ground for example.

15

Whiskers

You will need ten 4cm (1½in) lengths of horsetail hair. Make a hole in the side of the snout with your needle in the same way you did for the eyes. Insert one whisker into the hole. Then make four more holes in the same area. Insert all the whiskers, then add a tiny dab of glue to where they are inserted and leave it to dry. Repeat the same process on the other side.

Beechnut Children

I cannot walk through the woods, find empty beechnut shells and not make use of their lovely curly shape. They are perfect for hats and I have also popped a bead onto the stalk and made little beechnut gnomes!

SKILL LEVEL
Crafty beginner

FINISHED SIZE
5cm (2in)

TECHNIQUES USED
Shaping with wool,
adding features

1

Roll a pinch of your choice of main colour wool batt into an oblong shape of about 5 x 3cm (2 x 1¼in). Using your coarse felting needle (#36), felt the shape all over to make it firmer but also felt one end so that it becomes flat. Keep felting into the flat base until the shape shrinks down to 4cm (1½in) length. Make sure the other end is felted into a pointy shape.

2

Take your pink wool and wind flat strands of it around the pointy end of the shape. Use your medium felting needle to felt the wool down as you build the layers.

When the head measures about 1.5–2cm (½–¾in), felt into the top to round it off and felt all over the shape. Felt a groove for a neck where the body meets the head. Change to your fine needle to smooth out the wool. If the head shrinks too much, add more pink wool.

3

Now add more layers around the body shape, make sure you maintain the cone shape and slowly add more layers around the base.

This part will become the bell-shaped base. Next, only add more around the broad base away from the head and upper body.

4

Stand your shape up and felt it from the top down into the broad base. If it fastens on to your felting mat, gently lift the shape off at regular intervals and repeat, adding wool and felting into the base to make it broader and taller. You should be still using the coarse needle. Turn your shape over and stab from underneath to neaten the edges and keep the base concave. When the base measures 3cm (1¼in) and the figure is 4cm (1½in) tall it is time to stop.

5

Use your fine needle to felt tiny wisps of black for the eyes, and a tiny wisp of red for a mouth, onto the face. These wisps should be as small as you can possibly make them.

6

Hair

Take the green Bluefaced Leicester curls and cut the curliest strands free (do not pull them as they will become frizzy). Starting at the sides of the face, felt the curls into place on the head. Frame the face on both sides – mind out, as the curls can be quite unruly. Then cover the back of the head with curls and fit the beechnut hat.

Glue the hat down and apply pressure until the glue has dried so that it fits firmly onto the head. Make lots more beechnut children in different colours!

Seed Baby in a Walnut Shell

Autumn is a time of year when I feel a deep sadness that leaves, flowers and other plants are disappearing and the winter landscape is emerging, bleak and lifeless. Of course, life is far from gone; autumn is when seeds are nurtured and are getting ready to spring up again. It's reassuring to imagine that tiny seed babies are fast asleep in nut shells.

SKILL LEVEL
Crafty beginner
FINISHED SIZE
4–5cm (1½–2in)
TECHNIQUES USED
Shaping with wool, adding features

YOU WILL NEED

WOOL BATTS

1g (¹⁄₂₄oz) pink Australian Merino
1g (¹⁄₂₄oz) hare-brown Merino
1g (¹⁄₂₄oz) green variegated NZ Merino
Tiny wisps of black and red, or pink, wool

EXTRAS

Bluefaced Leicester curls in brown or white
Walnut halves

TOOLS

#38 medium felting needle
#40 fine felting needle
Felting mat
Scissors
PVA glue

1

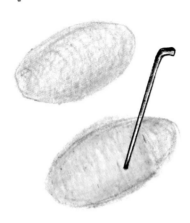

Roll a good pinch of the pink wool into a short little sausage of about 3 x 2cm (1¼ x ¾in). Then felt it down with your medium needle to firm it up. When your shape measures 2 x 1.5cm (¾ x ½in), wrap thin layers of the variegated green wool around it so that the shape is two-thirds covered in green.

2

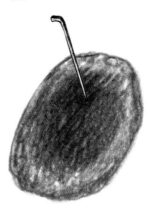

Take a good pinch of the hare-brown wool – enough to fit stuffed tightly into your walnut half. Felt the brown wool down to a smaller, tighter shape by folding the sides in and felting it flat on your mat, but not too flat.

Keep fitting it into the walnut half. It needs to fit tightly so that it can be wedged in there without falling out. Once it fits in that way put it to one side.

3

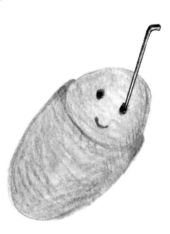

Use your fine felting needle to felt two tiny black dots onto the pink face for the eyes and one in red for a little mouth. Keep these as small as you can manage.

Hair

Take your tiny Bluefaced Leicester curls and separate them by cutting rather than tearing (tearing will make them frizzy). Pick the most suitable curls and gently felt them onto the head. Arrange the curls so that some loose locks fall into the face.

4

Felt the tiny baby onto the brown base by stabbing into the sides of the baby and into the base. Do this all the way around and then felt the base onto the baby from the back too. The two shapes will now be firmly attached to one another.

5

Finally, squeeze the baby into the walnut half. It should be wedged in there and you should not have to glue it down; however, if it falls out you could add a dab of glue

Acorn Children

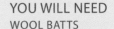

There are some beautiful books for children that depict little fairy folk in the woods. One of them is *Woody, Hazel and Little Pip* by Elsa Beskow. This was one of my children's favourite books and the little forest children characters caused mayhem and mischief. The Acorn Children here are inspired by this lovely story.

YOU WILL NEED

WOOL BATTS

2g (1/12oz) variegated green NZ Merino

1g (1/24oz) olive-green Australian Merino

1g (1/24oz) pink Australian Merino

1g (1/24oz) dark-brown Milk sheep

EXTRAS

Acorn cup

1m (39½) chestnut-brown boucle or mohair knitting yarn

1 x 36cm (14¼in) length #22 gauge paper-covered wire

TOOLS

#38 medium felting needle

#40 fine felting needle

Felting mat

Wire cutters or old scissors

PVA glue

SKILL LEVEL
Crafty beginner

FINISHED SIZE
8–10cm (3¹/₈–4in) tall

TECHNIQUES USED
Wrapping wire with wool, adding features and surface detail

1

Follow the instructions for the Small Basic Fairy Body on page 20, but when you get to covering the leg wire, do this with the variegated green wool, leaving 0.5cm (¼in) uncovered on each end.

Then cover the ends with the dark-brown wool, bend the wire over to trap the wool and wrap the foot tightly for about 2cm (¾in) before continuing with the brown wool up the leg, creating a candy-stripe effect.

2

Continue as described in the Small Basic Fairy Shape instructions, covering the whole body and upper arms with the variegated green wool.

3

Take two pinches of the olive-green wool and fold each one under at one end to make a neat, rounded edge. Lay one on the back of the figure so that the round edge is at the bottom, like a skirt hem.

Do the same with the second at the front. Use your medium felting needle to felt the wispy ends of the olive-green skirt halves into the upper body, allowing the fibres to softly melt into the variegated green cover.

4

Then stab the needle into the skirt at a shallow angle from the base upwards. This will help to shorten it. Make sure that the sides are joined together. Repeat to shorten and firm up the skirt. The round hem should stay in place.

5

Needle felting eyes and a mouth is optional. Keep the features small and remember to have the eyes in the centre line of the head. Use your fine needle for facial features.

6

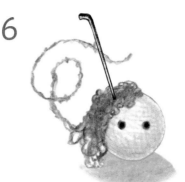

Take your hair yarn and stab the ends into the side of the head, continuing to add the hair as you go and concentrating on framing the face first. You do not need to cut short strands off.

When you get to the back of the head, make sure you do not stab your needle in too deeply as you will contaminate the face with brown fibres if they get pushed right through.

7

Take your acorn cup and fit onto the head like a cap and glue it into place. If the cup is a little small apply pressure until the glue has dried.

Toadstool House

Be honest, when you first saw this house, did you think, 'I wish I could live there!' This is the response I have heard from most people and, indeed, there is something so cosy and charming about a toadstool house that it seems unfair that it is reserved for fairy folk only.

YOU WILL NEED

WOOL BATTS

30g (1oz) cream, lanolin-rich core wool

15g (½oz) poppy-red NZ Merino

3g (⅛oz) bleached-white Australian Merino

3g (⅛oz) Gotland Island grey

3g (⅛oz) hare-brown Merino

1g (¹⁄₂₄oz) multicoloured fairy mix Merino/silk

1g (¹⁄₂₄oz) brown Portuguese Merino

1g (¹⁄₂₄oz) green variegated NZ Merino

1g (¹⁄₂₄oz) brown/grey South German Merino

1g (¹⁄₂₄oz) Stone sheep 'natural' black lamb

EXTRAS

1g (¹⁄₂₄oz) green Bluefaced Leicester Curls

1g (¹⁄₂₄oz) brown/grey Bluefaced Leicester Curls

TOOLS

#36 coarse felting needle

#38 medium felting needle

#40 fine felting needle

Three-needle multitool (optional)

Large felting mat minimum 20 x 20cm (8 x 8in)

Scissors

SKILL LEVEL
Crafty beginner

FINISHED SIZE
20cm (8in) long

TECHNIQUES USED
Basic shaping with wool, adding shapes and features

1

Stalk

Take half of your cream core wool and roll it into a sausage of about 14 x 8cm (5½ x 3⅛in). Using your medium felting needle, felt the wispy ends into the shape so that it holds together. Felt all over, as well as into, one end of the sausage to form a flat base – keep the edges soft and unfelted. Felt the base so that it curves inwards slightly; this will help the toadstool to stand up.

2

Take half of the remaining cream wool and wrap it around the main shape again. Felt this down so that it stays in place. Felt the base once again but leave the top unfelted.

3

Base

Take a good pinch off the remaining cream wool and flatten it out into a 10 x 12cm (4 x 5in) shape. If necessary, fold the sides in to achieve this size. Place your toadstool stump onto the soft base so that the wide part of the base is on the side. The stump itself is partially on the base towards the back.

4

Turn the whole arrangement over and felt the new flat part into the base of the toadstool. Then turn everything right way up and felt into the edge of the toadstool, working right through the flat base. Also begin felting the flat base flat to firm it up. If you have a three-needle multi tool, use it to speed this process up.

Add wisps of the cream wool, so that they cover the join between the stump and the flat base and build up the bulk. Felt the wisps down to create a smooth transition between stump and base. Keep some of the cream wool to one side for the window frame in the roof.

6

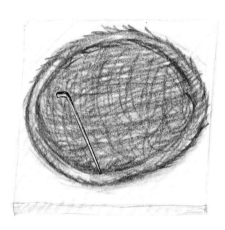

Roof

Take three quarters of the red wool and flatten it out into a 17 x 17cm (6¾ x 6¾in) piece. Place your wool on a felting mat. Take your coarse felting needle and felt the outline of a circle about 1cm (³⁄₈in) in from the edge. The diameter should be 16cm (6¼in). Fold the wispy ends inwards and felt them down inside the circle.

7

Take your red shape off the mat before it becomes too attached to it, then felt the shape from the same side again to fasten the fibres together a little more; however, the shape will mostly remain unfelted. Turn the shape over so that the tucked-in sides are underneath and place it on top of the toadstool stump.

8

Felt the red top onto the stump by stabbing into the red wool and slightly pulling the red shape over the sides of the stump. It is important that the length of the toadstool is retained, so if you find that it is getting squashed, give it a pull to stretch it out as the overall shape is still very soft. Keep working your way all around the red top. The shape should become more rounded. Stab into the sides to shrink them down so that it does not look ruffled.

9

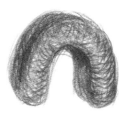

Window

Take enough of the remaining red wool so that you can roll it into a small shape, which measures about 10 x 6cm (4 x 2½in) and 3cm (1¼in) thick. Felt it down with a few stabs to secure the shape. Mould the shape into an arch using your hands. Maintaining the arch shape, felt it, using your coarse needle, until it is firmer. Keep the ends unfelted. The shape will shrink down as it firms up and should fit into your curved hand. The depth should be about 3cm (1¼in).

10

Place the arch onto the red top of the toadstool facing towards the extended base. Felt into the edges of the arch to attach it. Then continue fastening it on while shaping it. Stab straight into the rounded arch and fasten the wispy fibres at the ends into the red top. This is a dormer-style window that needs to face straight out rather than up or down. Stuff the window space with more red wool and felt it down so that it is firm and flat.

11

Add a layer of black wool over the red window. Felt it down with a curved top, and a straight base. Tease some cream wool into a thin strand. Felt this into the black window, to form a white window frame. Add a white cross in the centre of the window to form smaller windowpanes. Now adjust the shape of the toadstool if need be. You should still be able to adjust the shape as the toadstool overall will remain only softly felted.

12

Chimney

Take a wisp off the Gotland Island grey (the larger amount of pure grey) and put it to one side to use for pebbles later. Take the remaining grey wool and flatten it out into a square about 10 x 10cm (4 x 4in). Fold one side in by about 2cm (¾in). Roll the shape up so that the folded-in side is at one end of the sausage shape. This will form the top of the chimney.

13

Felt the grey sausage down into a rounded shape but leave the end that is unfolded unfelted. Now felt into the end with the folded edge and make an indentation of about 2cm (¾in) diameter. This will be the top of the chimney. Later the smoke will come out of this indentation.

14

Position the chimney on the red toadstool cap – slightly to the right of the dormer window – and felt the grey fibres in snugly so that they are close to the grey chimney and form a neat shape around the base. Once the chimney is fastened on you may need to adjust the shaping of the rest of the toadstool again.

15

Prepare the front of the toadstool for the front door and decoration by stabbing into it and flattening/firming this part up, especially where the door is going to go. From now on you will probably need to use your fine needle but change to medium if you're able.

16

Take the light brown (hare-brown Merino) and lay onto the front of the stump, then felt the outline of a door with a round top onto it. The door should measure about 6cm (2½in) tall and 5cm (2in) wide. Make sure the bottom of the door is straight. Then felt the wispy ends outside the line into the brown. Felt the door flat.

17

Take a small pinch of the dark brown wool (brown Portuguese Merino) and tease it into a strand. Felt this down as you go to form a door frame. In the same way, add three or four dark-brown vertical stripes to the door to give the impression of oak panelling.

18

To create a doorstep, take a small pinch of the brown-grey wool and felt it down below the door on the extended base. Now add a line of dark-brown wool at the bottom of the door as the final part of the doorframe.

19

Add a small window to the door in the same way as you did for the window in the roof. First add a little black patch – rounded at the top and straight on the sides and bottom. Then surround this with a line of the cream wool for a frame and a cross for dividing the windowpanes. Also add a doorknob in the brown-grey wool.

20

Take the variegated green wool and lay a wispy layer of it onto the front courtyard (the base) and felt it down so it looks like unruly grass.

21

Now make the little pebbles that lead to the front door. Use the leftover grey (used for the chimney), the brown-grey and any other colours you may have left, such as beige, hare brown, dark brown and black. Roll wisps of wool into a ball shape and felt them onto the grassy area by stabbing into the sides of the ball shape first. It is OK for them to sink into the grass. Pebbles should be about 1–1.5cm (³/₈–½in) in size. You can reduce the size by stabbing straight into them once they're fastened on.

22

You could mix the beige, browns and black to make a variegated colour. To do this, lay the chosen fibres on top of one another and tease them apart. Lay them on top of one another again, tease them apart and repeat until you have a new mottled colour. Vary the colours you mix to get a variety of pebbles. Add as many pebbles as you like.

24

23

Next felt your brown/grey curls to look like gnarled rosebush branches to frame the door. If you need to separate the curls use scissors to cut them rather than pulling them as they will turn frizzy. Add the green curls in the same way, weaving them in and out of the brown/grey curls. Next, take the multicoloured fairy mix and separate it into little wisps. Roll them into balls/ roses and felt them into the curls around the door.

Finally, use the white wool to add spots to the red cap by felting them on with your medium felting needle. Adjust the 'roof' as needed. To finish, shape a long strand of white wool that can be felted into the chimney pot to make smoke.

Large Gnome

This friendly gnome is gentle and cares for all the animals and plants that need a helping hand. He walks through the forest every day and, if you look carefully, you might find some tiny pointy boot prints.

SKILL LEVEL
Crafty beginner

FINISHED SIZE
22cm (8¾in) total height

TECHNIQUES USED
Wrapping wire with wool, basic shaping, adding shapes, and features

YOU WILL NEED

WOOL BATTS
15g (½oz) beige Fox sheep
5g (⅙oz) grey/brown Country sheep
4g (⅐oz) red variegated NZ Merino
2g (1/12oz) dark-brown Milk sheep
5g (⅙oz) variegated green NZ Merino
1g (1/24oz) white NZ Merino
Wisp of black NZ Merino

EXTRAS
Blusher (optional)
3g (⅛oz) brown/grey Bluefaced Leicester curls
2 x 6mm black glue-in eyes
2 x 30cm (12in) extra-strong pipe cleaners

TOOLS
#36 coarse felting needle
#38 medium felting needle
Scissors
PVA glue
Wire cutters or old scissors
Felting mat

1

Split your beige wool in half and put one half aside for later. Tease off a strand and wrap it around a pipe cleaner about 6cm (2½in) away from the end. Wrap the wool tightly and flat, like a ribbon. If you work closely to the shape and keep the wraps tight the wool should initially stick to itself. When the ball shape gets larger use your felting needle and felt it down. The finished size should be 4cm (1½in) in diameter.

Leave about 5cm (2in) at the top/head end of the pipe cleaner uncovered. This will become the poseable hat later.

2

Once you have completed the main shape, use a small ball of the same wool (about 1.5–2cm [½–¾in]) and felt it into the centre of the main shape. Felt the sides of the ball into the main shape before stabbing into the small ball itself – this keeps it round.

3

Repeat the process described in Step 2 with two slightly larger ball shapes positioned to the right and left. You now have a nose in the centre and chubby cheeks on either side. Take small pinches of beige wool and lay a couple on top of one another to create a wad. Place the wad onto the forehead and felt it down, still using your coarse needle, to build up this area.

4

Take another pinch of wool, flatten it, and lay it over the entire face (nose, cheeks, forehead). Initially, fasten this cover on at the sides, top and bottom (mind the wire), then follow the contours of the face. You should now have a smoother surface connecting the added facial features.

5

Arms

Take a strand of the beige wool and cut a 20cm (8in) length off a new pipe cleaner length. Begin wrapping the pipe cleaner with as thin a layer of wool as you can manage leaving just 0.5cm (⅛in) uncovered at the end. Bend the end of the pipe cleaner back by 1cm (³/₈in) and cover with the same wool to make a solid little hand (fist). Repeat this process on the other end of the pipe cleaner but leave about 1cm (³/₈in) uncovered in the centre.

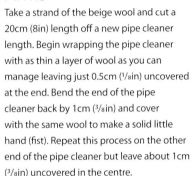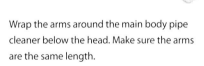

Wrap the arms around the main body pipe cleaner below the head. Make sure the arms are the same length.

6

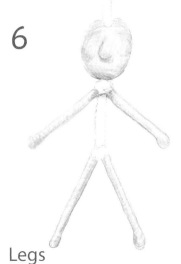

Legs

Cut 15cm (6in) of pipe cleaner off the main body and wrap it with wool as you did for the arms, but this time cover the whole length. Wind the main body pipe cleaner around the centre of the leg pipe cleaner to fasten it on. The distance between the head and the top of the legs should be 4cm (1½in).

7

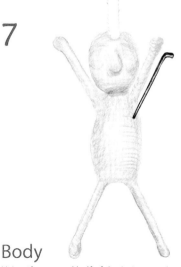

Body

Using the second half of the beige wool, take some strands and wrap them around the body, starting at the top. Bend the arms out of the way and felt the wool down as you go.

Be mindful of the wire. Keep building bulk around the tummy – do this by using the technique you used for the face: adding wads of wool, then do the same on the back but a little lower down so that you make his bottom stick out. His shape should be exaggerated.

8

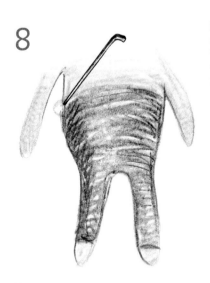

Trousers

Take the grey/brown wool and start wrapping it around the legs to give the gnome trousers. Then cover the second leg and continue wrapping up around the body, the bottom and halfway up the tummy. Your gnome should now have trousers.

9

Boots

Take the dark-brown wool and wrap the end of each leg with thin, tight layers of it to make boots. Continue wrapping the brown wool about 1–2cm (³/₈–¾in) beyond the end of the pipe cleaner. Then felt it down – the part without a wire inside needs to be felted flat. Now bend the foot part at a right angle to the leg and use your needle to establish this shape by stabbing into the bend from the top and the base.

10

Red top

Take the red wool and flatten it into a shape that fits on the palm and fingers of your hand. Make a hole in the centre of it. Slip the red shape over the gnome's head and adjust it with your fingers so that it looks like a cape, covering the arms and the front and back of the body.

11

Using your coarse felting needle, felt in a straight and consistent line just underneath the arm. The idea is to join the two sides of the red cape and create a seam under the arm. Turn the gnome over and do the same from the back. Repeat this on the other arm.

Take your sharp scissors and cut into the red wool just below the seams you have felted shut. Repeat on the other side.

12

You will now have a sleeve that is closed but two open sides on either side of the body. Take an open side from the back and fold it under the open side at the front. Then fold the front over the back and felt it down. Repeat on the other side. This will also fasten the red top onto the upper body. Leave the bottom fibres loose for now.

13

Next, tidy the sleeves and seams using your felting needle to stab the seams flat. Tidy the ends of both sleeves by stabbing into the space between the arms and sleeves to tuck the wispy fibres in. Fold the bottom of the top in so that you can neaten that area also. Felt the folded edge to secure it. Repeat on the other side. Make sure you do not fasten the very end of the top onto the trousers but leave about 1cm (³/₈in) hanging loose.

14

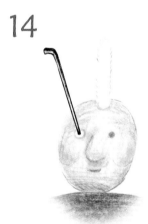

Features
Return to the head of the gnome and felt indentations on either side of the nose for eye sockets. Make a line for the mouth too. Add a little white wool into the eye sockets.

15

Take your coarse needle and insert it into the centre of the white wool in the eye until the thicker part of the needle goes in. This will make a hole. Take the needle out and immediately insert the pin of the black glue-in eye. Repeat on the other side. Add a dab of glue behind the eye without taking it out. Push it firmly back in. Then repeat on the other side.

16

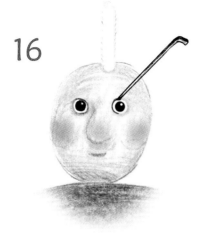

Take a tiny wisp of the dark-brown wool you used for the boots and shape it into a strand by twisting it between your fingers. Felt around the eye (leaving the white to show) like eyeliner. Repeat on the other side. Add a little blusher to make the cheeks and nose rosy.

17

Beard

Take your Bluefaced Leicester curls and sort through them making sure you have separated strands of the correct length – a maximum of 10cm (4in). Use your scissors to separate the curls as pulling them apart will only make them frizzy. Fasten a strand of curl to the side of the face to start the beard.

Then work your way around the base of the face, adding more curls but leaving the mouth area uncovered. Use a short length of curl to felt a small moustache just under the nose. Continue adding shorter curls around the back of the gnome's neck where they will peek out from under the hat.

18

Hat

Take the green wool and start wrapping the top end of the pipe cleaner. As with the hands and feet, bend the end of the pipe cleaner over. You will need to cover all the pipe cleaner but also beyond it to make the hat about 8cm (3¹⁄₈in) tall. Felt the layers down as you go.

19

When you get to the top of the head, felt the green wool on but keep the edges wispy. Begin shaping the hat and extending the top by about 2–3cm (¾–1¼in). The edges of the hat will need to be shaped in the same way as the hem of the red top. So, fold the wool under and felt just above the edge.

20

At some point you will need to start adding patches of the green wool rather than wrapping layers. Make sure you felt these down and add wispy covers if you need to hide a join. The hat can come down further on the back of the head. To finish off, felt into the gap between the hat and the head. You can bend the wire inside the hat to give it a jaunty angle.

Small Gnome

This gnome is a little busy helper in the forest. His job is to tidy away pinecones, especially in the autumn when many of them need to be put in store to help feed the Wood Mouse and others when little food is available. He also has a much better memory than the forgetful squirrels.

SKILL LEVEL
Crafty beginner
FINISHED SIZE
12cm (4in) to top of hat
TECHNIQUES USED
Wrapping wool around wire, adding shapes and features

YOU WILL NEED
WOOL BATTS
2g (¹/₁₂oz) green raindrops NZ Merino
2g (¹/₁₂oz) dragon NZ Merino
2g (¹/₁₂oz) pink Australian Merino
1g (¹/₂₄oz) natural black Stonesheep lamb
1g (¹/₂₄oz) fox-red variegated NZ Merino

EXTRAS
1 x 36cm (14¼in) length #22 gauge paper-covered wire
1g (¹/₂₄oz) brown/grey Bluefaced Leicester curls
Blusher (optional)

0TOOLS
#38 medium felting needle
#40 fine felting needle
Felting mat
Wire cutters or old scissors
PVA glue

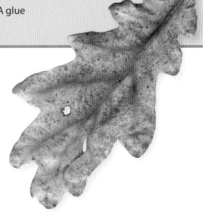

Cut your 36cm (14¼in) length of paper-
covered wire into three equal parts of 12cm
(4¾in) each.

1

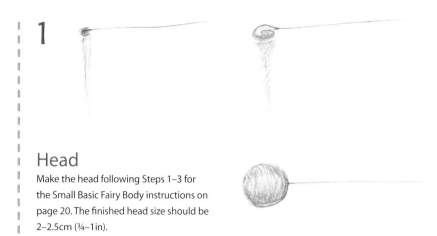

Head

Make the head following Steps 1–3 for
the Small Basic Fairy Body instructions on
page 20. The finished head size should be
2–2.5cm (¾–1in).

2

Nose

Take a small amount of the same wool and
roll it tightly into a ball (small pea size) –
give this a few stabs just to hold the shape
together. Felt the pea-size ball onto the
middle of the head shape where the face
will be. Do this by stabbing your fine needle
into the edge of the small ball and the head.
This way you will not flatten the nose. Once
you have fastened the nose on you can stab
into the shape directly to neaten it up or
make it smaller if needed.

3

Take a pinch of the pink and keep it flat
like a sheet. Lay this over the face so that it
covers the nose and face. Felt down around
the edges but keep the cover on the face
taut. You should still be using your fine
felting needle. Felt all over following the
shape of the face. You should now have an
overly large nose in the middle of the face.

4

Eyes

Make indentations for the eyes on either
side of the upper part of the nose. Felt tiny
black spots into the indentations using the
natural black wool.

5

Arms

Make the arms following Step 4 for the Small Basic Fairy Body instructions on page 22. Bend the end of the wire in by 0.5cm (1/8in) to make the fists. Use the green raindrops wool to add more bulk to the arms, starting at one wrist and wrapping wool layers along the arms. Cover the whole area between the hands evenly. If you keep the wool tight you should not need to needle felt the arm at all at this stage.

6

Legs

Take the last length of wire and wrap it with the dragon wool mix, starting 1cm (3/8in) in from the end of the wire and leaving the same length bare at the other end. Again, add glue to help the wool to grip; however, this time the wire ends do not need to be bent in yet. Add more layers of wool, building up more bulk around the lower leg area and use your fine felting needle to felt it down.

7

Shoes

Take your natural black wool and cover one end of the wire thinly. Then bend it in by 1cm (3/8in). Make sure the bend is covered in black. Cover the parallel running wires at the bend and felt the black wool on the wire end down.

8

Bend 1cm (3/8in) of the black wire end in at a 90-degree angle; this should make it look like a shoe. Work on shaping this area by making the end pointier and the base flat.

You could add more black wool to make a longer boot, but this is optional. Repeat on the other side to make the other shoe, then bend the leg wire in half with the feet pointing in the same direction.

9

Next, the legs and arms need to be fastened to the body. First, bend your main body wire 3cm (1¼in) down from the base of the head. Trap the centre of the legs in the upward bend of the main body wire.

Twist the main body wire around the centre of the legs, leaving the main body wire pointing up.

Trap the arms between the two parallel main body wires and twist the loose end around the centre of the arms as you did with the legs. Make sure the sharp end is tucked in.

10

Next, take the dragon mix wool and wrap the lower part of the body. It helps to move the arms upwards and out of the way. Make sure you wrap some of the same wool around the centre of the legs so that all the wire is covered. Then felt down.

11

Now, cover the upper body below the arms with the green raindrops wool and continue downward, overlapping the dragon mix wool slightly. Then felt down. Add thinner strands of the green wool around the tops of the arms and neck and continue under the arms. Felt it all into place. Build up layers of wool on the arms because the next step will make the top appear baggier, so the arms need to look bulkier.

12

Take a pinch of the green wool, roughly as long as the gnome from neck to foot. Fold this piece under at one end to make a neat edge and place it on the gnome's chest, so that the wispy ends face up. The folded edge should protrude over the legs but not cover them entirely. Felt the wispy ends at the top into the neck and upper chest of the gnome. Continue downwards but keep the stabs shallow so that the green top looks looser than before.

13

Use another pinch of the green wool to repeat the process on the back. Make sure that the two sides fuse into one another. Push the arms out of the way as required. If needed, cover any gaps or joins with a wisp of green wool and felt it down.

14

Beard and hair

Cut strands from the Bluefaced Leicester curls, rather than pulling (this will make them frizzy). Begin felting the curls onto the gnome's face, just below the nose and reaching to where you imagine the ears to be. Use your fine or medium needle. You can shorten the beard by stabbing your needle upwards from the beard towards the nose. This will pull the fibres in and shorten them. Next, take shorter off-cuts and felt them along the forehead. These will poke out from under the hat. Do the same around the neck part of the gnome at the back. Do not worry if you have a bald patch on the back of the head as this will be covered by the hat.

15

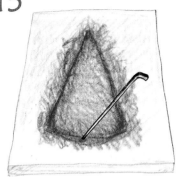

Hat

Take a good pinch of the fox-red variegated wool and keep it flat; it should measure about 8 x 8cm (3¹⁄₈ x 3¹⁄₈in). Lay it on your felting mat and 'draw' the outline of a triangle with a curved base on it with your felting needle. The straight sides should be 7cm (2¾in) long. The distance between the end of the first side and the other should also be 7cm (2¾in); however, in reality it will be longer because you will felt it into a curved shape.

16

Felt the wispy sides in from outside the line. Do not felt down too much though because you will need to lift the shape off your mat before it fastens on. Once lifted off the mat, keep working on felting the shape into a firmer fabric – do this from both sides. If you have any holes or thin patches add a little extra wool.

17

Once it feels like a firm fabric, fold the shape in half so that the two straight sides meet, and the curved edge is at the bottom. Using your medium needle, felt into both straight edges to join them together. Felt from both sides to make a solid seam less than 0.5cm (¹⁄₈in) from the bottom edge. You should be able to fit the hat onto your finger.

18

Fit the hat onto the gnome's head with the seam at the back. Initially, felt the hat onto the top of the gnome's head: keep the edge of the hat open for now. Neaten the edge of the hat by stabbing your needle into the space between the hat and the curly hair.

This will tuck away hat fibres and keep the two – hat and head – separate. Do this all the way around. To shape and/or shorten the hat use your medium felting needle to stab into the hat from the top down. This will give it a crumpled look. You can also stab into the back seam to neaten it.

19

To finish, you could add a little blusher to your gnome's nose to give him a little more colour in his face. Then, place a small pinecone into his arms to finish him off.

Large Fawn

If you are ever lucky enough to stumble upon a fawn during a walk in the forest, it will be very tempting to get close. You may even think this fawn has been abandoned by its mum. Fawns, however, are often left while their mother goes to find food, so leave well alone, especially if the fawn is lying down just obediently waiting for its mum's return.

YOU WILL NEED

WOOL
50g (1¾oz) of off-white basic core wool batts
56g (2oz) of cream lanolin-rich core batts
20g (²/₃oz) of brown Manx Loaghtan tops
3g (¹/₈oz) of natural white NZ Merino batts
1g (¹/₂₄oz) of black NZ Merino batts
1g (¹/₂₄oz) of light-yellow NZ Merino batts

EXTRAS
36cm (14¼in) green stem wire

TOOLS
#38 medium felting needle
#36 coarse felting needle
Felting mat
PVA glue
Wire cutters
Scissors
Small or medium carding brush (optional)
Three-needle multitool (optional)

IDENTIFY THE DIFFERENT WHITE WOOLS
- Basic core wool: Off-white, quite 'bitty', may contain natural vegetation.
- Lanolin-rich core: Cream in colour, feels 'sticky', may contain natural vegetation.
- Natural White NZ Merino: The whitest wool with even fibres.

SKILL LEVEL
Beginner to advanced

FINISHED SIZE
25cm (10in) long

TECHNIQUES USED
Making basic shapes, joining shapes, adding details

1

Head

Start with the creamier coloured lanolin-rich core wool. Split this wool into two and put one half of it aside. Take your first half of cream, lanolin-rich core wool and split it into half again, about 15g (½oz), and roll it into a ball shape by winding it up on itself. It works best if you keep stretching the wool out so that it can be wrapped around the shape as many times as possible, making the outside smooth and neat.

2

Once you have teased the fibres out and around the shape as much as possible, use your medium needle to stab into the main shape to secure it. Stab the ball shape all over to firm it up and make it nice and round. It should be about the size of a tennis ball, 7cm (2¾in) in diameter. See template below for size.

3

Next, take about one third of the left-over half of cream, lanolin-rich core wool, keep it flat and then fold it in half with the folded edge at the top. Then roll the folded sheet inwards from the side into a sausage shape. This will become the snout of the fawn. Felt the shape closed. Then stab along one end for about 2–3cm (¾in–1¼in) to reduce it in size and make the snout more conical.

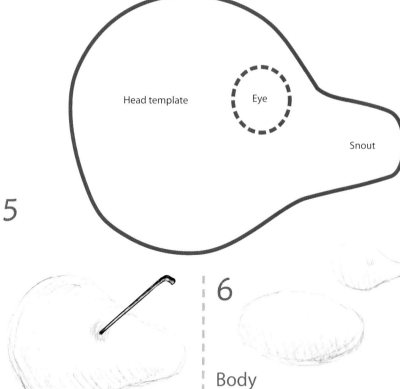

Head template

Eye

Snout

4

The fibres at the wider part are left unfelted. Tease these fibres out so that they become an open shape which can fit onto the head. Tear off any excess if necessary. Fit the snout onto the round head shape and felt the loose end fibres into place. Make sure you pull the snout tightly onto the head so that it is firmly attached. Measure this against the template above and adjust accordingly.

5

Take a thin layer of the same wool, about the size of your hand – note that it is almost transparent. Lay this over the snout and, reaching over the head, felt it down. Do not add bulk, just firm up the shape. With your needle, make two indentations for the eyes.

6

Body

Take the basic core wool (the off-white 'bitty' wool) and split it into three parts. Use one third, about 15g (½oz), to make a shape like the one you made for the head but more oblong. Use your coarse needle to stab the wispy ends in and to firm it up a little. The illustration (above) shows the comparison in size between the head and body.

7

Then split another third of the wool into two. Use one part (about 7–8g [¼oz]) to add a layer of wool onto the body and felt it down. Repeat this with the other part (another 7–8g [¼oz]). The body should now be three times the size of the head. Put the remaining basic core wool aside.

8

Legs

Take the green stem wire and the second half of the creamy, lanolin-rich core wool (28g [1oz]) that you set aside for the legs at the start. Split this into four equal portions, 7g (¼oz) each. Take a small strand from one and start wrapping the wispy end around the wire about 16–17cm (6¼–6¾in) along.

9

The wire is a means of making a leg shape by wrapping the wool around it and then pulling the wire out leaving you with a tight leg shape. You will use the whole length of the wire though only wrapping about half of the length with wool. The trick is to keep the wool flat like a ribbon and to keep adding thin, tight layers until the leg measures 17–18cm (6¾–7in) long and 2.5cm (1in) thick. Do not use glue or any wax to help with the wrapping as you will slip the shape off the wire once it is thick enough. The leg should be firm (the more layers of thin wool used, the firmer the leg will be), with no need to felt it down, though you can tidy one end (the foot) by stabbing into it a few times. You will use all the allocated wool (7g [¼oz]) per leg.

10

Hind leg   Front leg

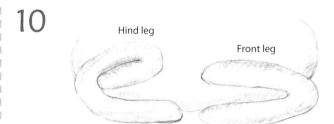

Make four legs. Then fasten the front leg onto one side of the body by bending it roughly in half and only stabbing into the top part onto the body with your medium needle.

The hind leg is folded twice and the top part will become the hip area, so felt it onto the side of the body with as small a gap between the bend as possible. Attach the other two legs on the opposite side.

11

To attach the head to the body, you need about 15cm (6in) of green stem wire. Insert this length into the head. You should be able to wriggle it in. Add a little glue into the hole. The wire will reach all the way into the head but ensure it does not poke out at the top. Now take a strand of the leftover cream, lanolin-rich core and wrap it around the wire at the base of the head. Felt the wool down around the wire and onto the base of the head with your medium needle. Note: You need to keep 3 x 1g (¹⁄₂₄oz) portions of this wool for the ears and tail, so don't use it all.

12

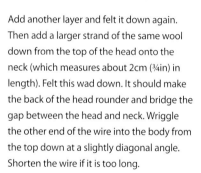

Add another layer and felt it down again. Then add a larger strand of the same wool down from the top of the head onto the neck (which measures about 2cm (¾in) in length). Felt this wad down. It should make the back of the head rounder and bridge the gap between the head and neck. Wriggle the other end of the wire into the body from the top down at a slightly diagonal angle. Shorten the wire if it is too long.

13

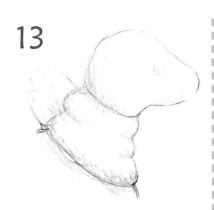

Take another strand of the cream, lanolin-rich core and wrap it around the neck like a scarf, but mostly overlapping the part of the body where the wire is inserted. Felt this down.

14

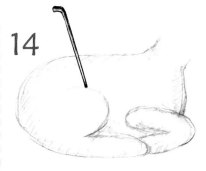

Using the basic core wool that you used to make the body, take a wad about the size of your hand to bulk out the chest. Lay it onto the fawn's front and felt it down with your coarse needle. Then take another wad of a similar size and lay it over the back of the fawn so it covers the top of the hind legs and felt this down as well. The double bend on the hind leg becomes one large hip area.

15

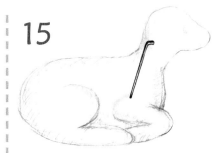

Use a slightly smaller portion of the same wool to cover the top of the front leg on one side first. Felt it down so that you can see the detail of the shoulder (top of the leg). Repeat this on the other side. The basic shape of your fawn is now complete. If you need to tweak it here and there, do so now. The head is now fixed but still poseable.

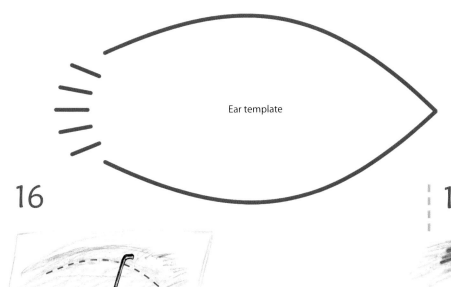

Ear template

16

Ears

You put aside 3 x 1g (¹/₂₄oz) portions of the cream, lanolin-rich core wool earlier. Use two of these portions for the ears. Take one and lay it flat on your felting mat. With your medium needle, stab the outline of the ear onto the flat piece of wool (see above).

Then fold the wispy ends inwards and felt them down except for one end – keep this unfelted. If needed, add a little more bulk to the inside of the ear and felt it all over. Keep lifting it off your mat to stop it fastening on to it.

17

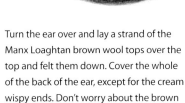

Turn the ear over and lay a strand of the Manx Loaghtan brown wool tops over the top and felt them down. Cover the whole of the back of the ear, except for the cream wispy ends. Don't worry about the brown coming through on the inside.

18

From the inside, shape the ear a little more by stabbing into the outer part but keeping the edge rounded.

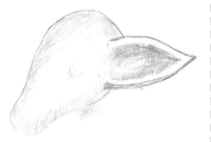

Spread the cream, wispy ends out and place the ear onto the side of the head, sticking out at a right angle for now. Felt it on to the head very lightly.

19

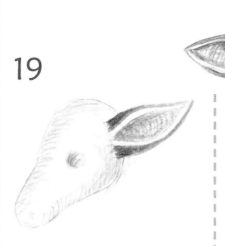

Pinch the ear in at the base and felt in from the sides with your felting needle to make a shell shape. Make a second ear in the same way. We will come back to the ears later.

20

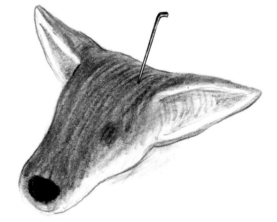

Nose

Take a pinch of the black wool and roughly shape it into a triangle with your hands. Lay it onto the front of the face and felt it down with your medium needle but make the point at the bottom flat and straight (a trapezoid shape).

21

From now on you will be using the brown tops, yellow batts, black batts, the natural white NZ Merino (that you have not yet used) and a combination of these fibres to colour the fawn. Mix the colours by hand or use small carders. Start by mixing the brown tops with a tiny amount of yellow to brighten up the brown and make it more golden. Mix the wool fibres by laying them on top of one another, then tearing them apart. Repeat this process until the colours are evenly mixed.

22

It is important that you lay the wool down on the fawn in the direction of the natural growth of the fur. In this way, colour in the face from the top of the head to the nose, mixing small batches of colour. Add a little black into the mix to cover the top of the snout and the muzzle. Cover the whole of the head, including where the eyes will go but keep the indentation for the eyes at the side of the head, about halfway between the ears and the nose. Keep the side of the head and around the eyes lighter in colour. If the white from the core wool is showing through it helps to keep the covering appear light. You may find yourself switching from the medium to the coarse needle and vice versa during the colouring-in process; use whatever works best for you.

23

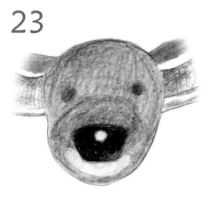

Take a small strand of the cream, lanolin-rich core (if still available; otherwise any of the other white wool will do) and felt a round lip onto the base of the nose. You can pre-shape the wool with your hands before felting it on. Cover the lip with a light mix of mostly white and a little brown. Felt it down so that it blends into the rest of the face cover. Add a tiny wisp of that same mix onto the front of the nose as a reflection highlight. It will look strange to start with but later will just seem natural.

24

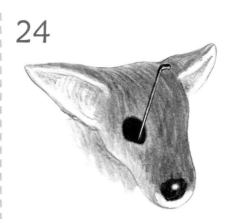

Eyes

Use a pinch of the black wool and lay it straight onto the indentation of one of the eyes. Start by felting down the outline of the eye. Fawns have huge eyes in comparison to their head. Make sure that the cover of black is even and has no thin patches.

Then take the same light mix you used for the bottom lip and make an eyelid by laying the wool loosely above the eye and then felting it down without reducing the size of the eye.

25

Use the brown tops to add a little line in front of the eye for a tear duct. Make a lower eyelid in the same way as you did for the upper eyelid, and then add a tiny spot of white onto the eye itself as a reflection highlight.

26

If you wish to add eyelashes, use a wisp of the black wool and felt it loosely onto the top of the eye, underneath the lid, then trim with scissors to shorten and neaten the lashes. Make the second eye to match the first. Make sure that you constantly compare the eyes and look at the fawn directly from the front to ensure the eyes are symmetrical.

27

Next, make a very light brown mix (white, brown and yellow) and lay it lengthways onto the chest and felt it down in that direction.

28

Tail

In real life fawns have quite large tails but because ours is lying down we will make it a little shorter. Take the final 1g (($^1/_{24}$oz)) portion of cream, lanolin-rich core and a strand of brown/white/yellow mix and lay them on top of one another. Give it a few stabs on your felting mat before attaching it to the back of the fawn with the white side underneath. Keep it shaggy. Don't worry about the join, it will be covered next.

29

Cover the fawn's back, starting at the bottom end, with a brown/white mix (we will add spots at the very end so keep it mostly brown). Use the same mix to cover the hip, thigh and shoulder over the legs, working in the natural growth direction of the fur. Imagine the fawn standing up, so the fur would run from the top of the leg downwards.

30

Hooves

Make a clean line between the black and white, then felt the black down over the foot part. Add unmixed brown tops to the leg above the hoof by blending in the wispy ends first. Felt them down next to the black with no white showing. Colour in the lower parts of all four legs in this way.

31

The fawn is lying down so you do not need to colour in the underside. You can now decide how the lower legs should be arranged and which side of the fawn looks the best. Firm up the ears by stabbing into their bases and finalise the position (slightly pointing up). Then add a little of the white wool you used for mixing to make them furrier on the inside. Felt the white so it reaches over the edge, then trim with scissors.

32

Finally, add spots onto the fawn's back and the tops of the legs, either in white, a white/yellow mix or both. Then felt the head into its final position by stabbing along the neck to firm it up.

Air

Rainbow Fairy

Rainbows are just magical, a perfect combination of colours all put together by nature itself. Rainbows also remind me of the days when my children were in kindergarten and on their birthdays the story was told of how they handed their angel wings to an older angel in heaven to be looked after and they came down the rainbow slide to be with their family. At the end of life, they would get their wings back – such a touching vision!

SKILL LEVEL
Crafty beginner
FINISHED SIZE
18cm (7in) long
TECHNIQUES USED
Wire wrapping and a little needle felting

YOU WILL NEED
WOOL
5g (¹⁄₆oz) standard core/stuffing batts
4g (¹⁄₇oz) pink South American Merino tops
4g (¹⁄₇oz) bleached-white Australian Merino batts
5g (¹⁄₆oz) rainbow Australian Merino tops
3g (¹⁄₈oz) white mohair tops

EXTRAS
2 x 30cm (12in) extra-strong pipe cleaners
15 x 15cm (6 x 6in) piece of rainbow tulle fabric with sparkly dots
2g (¹⁄₁₂oz) of Rainbow Sparkly Stuff
15cm (6in) length of rainbow sequin trim
1m (39½in) of extra-strong thread
1m (39½in) of silky thread
20cm (8in) length of blue embroidery thread
1 x small glass bottle with cork

TOOLS
#38 medium felting needle
Sewing or embroidery needle
Pliers
Scissors
Felting mat (optional)

1

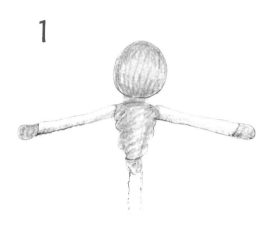

Make a base shape according to the Large Basic Fairy Body instructions on page16. Note that in Step 4 (page 18) of these instructions you should use a 16–18cm (6¼–7in) length of pipe cleaner, so use the second pipe cleaner and cut it to length. Use the bleached white Australian Merino batts to make the arms.

2

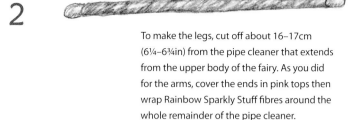

To make the legs, cut off about 16–17cm (6¼–6¾in) from the pipe cleaner that extends from the upper body of the fairy. As you did for the arms, cover the ends in pink tops then wrap Rainbow Sparkly Stuff fibres around the whole remainder of the pipe cleaner.

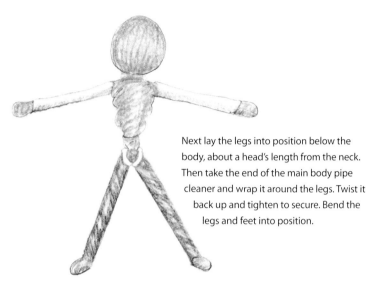

Next lay the legs into position below the body, about a head's length from the neck. Then take the end of the main body pipe cleaner and wrap it around the legs. Twist it back up and tighten to secure. Bend the legs and feet into position.

3

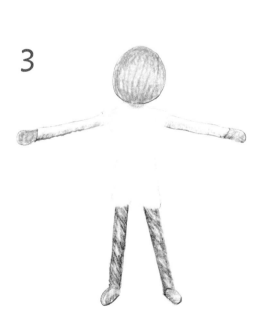

Use the bleached white batts (that you used for the arms) to wrap and secure the legs further, but also to give the fairy a white bodice. Felt it down gently to keep it looking fluffy.

4

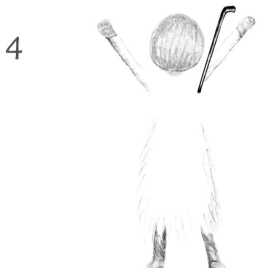

Take a good pinch of the same white batts, keep it flat and tear a hole in the middle. Slip this over the head of the fairy so that it reaches just below the waist. If the piece is too large or thick, take it off and shorten it or make it thinner by separating parts off it.

Use your felting needle to gently stab into the upper body to make the white batts a closer fit and to create short sleeves for the fairy. Keep your stabs shallow and be mindful of your fingers!

5

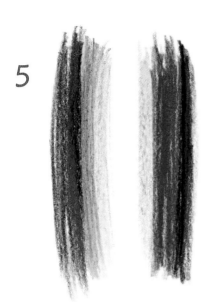

6

Skirt

Split your rainbow tops in half so that you end up with two shorter lengths of a maximum 5cm (2in) width each. To do this, gently pull the length apart, allowing the wool fibres to 'slither away' from one another rather than tearing it by holding the ends too tightly. You will only see four colours on each side facing up. Have one facing one way, the other the other way.

Lay one strand of rainbow tops onto the front of the fairy with the central part over the waist. Then lay the other half on the back of the fairy but with the other side facing out. By doing this you capture the full rainbow colour range.

Tease the two strands sideways so that they almost meet at the fairy's sides. Take a 20 x 0.5cm (8 x ¼in) thick strand of the Rainbow Sparkly Stuff fibre and tie it around the waist, just under the arms of the fairy. Pull it tight and secure with a knot.

7

Pull the tops that are above the waist down to form the skirt. Adjust it by spreading the tops evenly around the fairy, closing the small gap on each side. Cut the skirt short (including the fluffy white underskirt) so that the legs are visible. You can keep the skirt wispy, rather than bluntly cut – if you prefer you can shorten it by tearing wisps off the ends.

8

You can adjust the skirt further by cutting more off or by making it a little longer again by gently pulling the fibres down. Once you're happy with it, felt into the top area of the skirt to define the waist a little more.

9

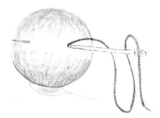

Eyes

If you want to give your fairy eyes, thread the blue embroidery strand onto a needle and secure it at the back of the head, then sew through to the front of the face to where the first eye will be. Go back and forth a couple of times – do not pull the thread too tightly. Then guide the needle underneath the face to where the second eye will be and repeat. Come out at the back of the head and secure your thread again. Don't worry if the back looks a little messy as it will be covered with hair.

10

Hair

Take your white mohair strand and tie the ends with a wispy thread of the Rainbow Sparkly Stuff to create hair bunches. You can trim the ends beyond the hair ties if you like or keep them wispy. Make sure that the length of hair between the hair ties fits comfortably over the fairy's head. Secure the hair by first stabbing into the top of the first tied bunch and head, then repeat this on the other side.

11

Pull the hair down the back of the fairy's head and felt it on at the neck only.

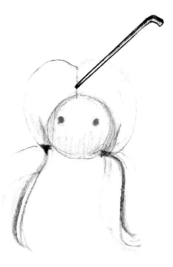

Finally felt along the top of the hair where you imagine the parting would be and felt a line all the way from the front to the back of the head. If the hair is wavy and loose that is fine.

12

Use the rainbow sequin trim to make a headband. You should have enough to tie it up at the back. You will not need to knot it as the sequins will grip onto one another. Alternatively, you could use the sequin trim to put around the fairy's waist.

13

Wings

Take the length of the rainbow tulle fabric and use scissors to round the corners off along the short ends. Then use the silk thread to tie it up in the centre. You will need a long enough tail of thread left to thread your sewing needle and use it to sew the wings onto the back of the fairy.

14

Fill the little glass bottle with Rainbow Sparkly Stuff. You may need a skewer, or similar, to fill the bottle. Make sure some fibres protrude out of the top. When you fasten the bottle with the cork it should look as though the rainbow is bursting out of the bottle. Pose your fairy holding on to her bottle and she is complete!

Forget-Me-Not Fairy

This little fairy is an Air fairy because she stands for all the memories of friends long gone. Forget-me-nots always remind me of the passing of a baby girl of a friend who only stayed on Earth for a few days after she was born. Forget-me-not flowers were blooming everywhere!

YOU WILL NEED

WOOL
5g (1/6oz) standard core batts,
5g (1/6oz) light-yellow NZ Merino batts
South American Merino tops:
   6g (1/5oz) pink
   5g (1/6oz) forget-me-not blue
   5g (1/6oz) cream

EXTRAS
1g (1/24oz) mermaid blue Angelina fibre
5 x fabric flowers
2 x 30cm (12in) extra-strong pipe cleaners
1m (39½in) of extra-strong thread,
50cm (19¾in) of silky thread
20cm (8in) length of blue embroidery thread

TOOLS
#38 medium felting needle
Sewing needle
PVA glue
pliers
Scissors
An iron
Parchment or greaseproof paper
Blue waterproof pen
Felting mat (optional)

SKILL LEVEL
Crafty beginner
FINISHED SIZE
20cm (8in) long or
15cm (6in) sitting
TECHNIQUES USED
Wire wrapping and
a little needle felting

1

Make a basic fairy shape by following the Large Basic Fairy Body instructions on page 16. Note that in Step 4 (page 18) you should use a 16–18cm (6¼–7in) length of pipe cleaner, so use the second pipe cleaner to cut to size. Use the pink wool tops to make the arms.

2

Legs

Measure and cut off about 16–17cm (6¼–6¾in) of the pipe cleaner that extends from the upper body of the fairy. Wrap the pink wool tops around each end leaving about 1cm (³/₈in) of wire exposed at the ends. Take a wisp of the forget-me-not blue colour and wrap one of the white ends thinly. Then bend it inwards, making sure that the bend is covered (as you did with the hands).

3

Continue wrapping the bend. Once you have covered about 2cm (¾in), wrap the last wispy ends of the blue around the leg like a candy stripe. If you have too much blue tear some off so that you only have just enough to make the laces.

Repeat on the other side and bend the legs in half. Also bend about 1cm (³/₈in) of the foot in so that you now have little, blue-covered feet.

4

Next lay the legs into position below the body – about a head's length away from the head. Use the spare pipe cleaner to secure the legs to the body by wrapping it around the 'crotch' and secure around the upper body. Use pinches of the light-yellow wool batts to wrap around the lower body. This will further secure the legs.

5

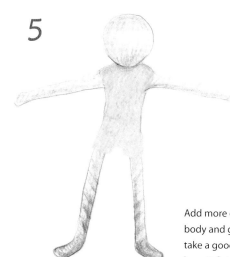

Add more of the yellow to fill out the upper body and give the fairy yellow bloomers. Then take a good pinch of the same yellow batt, keep it flat and tear a hole in the middle.

6

Slip the light-yellow shape over the fairy's head so that it hangs just below the waist. If it is too large or too thick, take it off, and either shorten or make it thinner by separating parts. Use your felting needle to gently stab into the upper body to make the yellow a closer fit and to create short sleeves for the fairy. You should not need a felting mat for this if you stab at an angle and keep your stabs shallow. Mind your fingers!

7

Next take one strand of the forget-me-not blue wool top; just a little longer than the fairy itself. Split the strand in half. At this point you could add a little of the Angelina fibre: it is primarily used for the wings but there will be enough left if you want to mix a few strands in with the skirt by laying the individual strands onto the blue wool.

Lay one half of the blue tops on the front of the fairy so that the legs are exposed, and the strand reaches over the head. Turn the fairy over and lay the second strand onto the back, in the position as for the front. Next, take a thin strand of wool top about 20cm (8in) long (whatever you have left; pink, yellow or blue) and tie it around the waist tightly.

8

Pull the skirt down (the tie will be underneath the waist and not visible) and adjust it by spreading it around the fairy, though there will be a small gap on each side. If necessary, shorten the skirt by gently teasing ends off (take care not to pull it off the fairy) and twisting the ends between your fingers about five to six times.

9

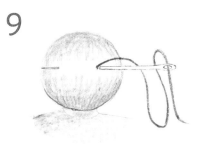

Eyes

If you want to give your fairy eyes, thread the blue embroidery strand onto a needle and secure it at the back of the head, then sew through to the front of the face to where the first eye will be. Go back and forth a couple of times – do not pull the thread too tightly. Then guide the needle underneath the face to where the second eye will be and repeat. Come out at the back of the head and secure your thread again.

10

Hair

Take all the cream wool tops and split one end into three strands. Ask somebody to hold the one end or pin it down as you plait the strands neatly. Tie a small strand of wool top around the plait to secure it (blue or any other colour you like). Cut the cream ends off or keep them wispy, whatever you prefer. Repeat on the other side but make sure than you have a good 4–5cm (1½–2in) of unplaited wool in between.

11

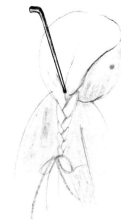

Broaden out the middle part of the hair so that it fits onto the fairy's head. Don't be afraid to put it down with a little force. Felt the hair onto the head with your needle along the middle, which will give the

appearance of a centre parting. Then pull each side down and felt by stabbing into the creases of the plait so that the rest of the hair stays unfelted.

12

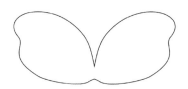

Wings

First fold your parchment paper in half, then open it out again. Lay one half of your paper over the wing template so that you can still see the template through it (see left). You may wish to trace the template onto a blank piece of paper first. Take small wisps of Angelina fibre and lay these on top of the parchment, following the shape of the wing. Do this on both wings.

Parchment sits on top of template

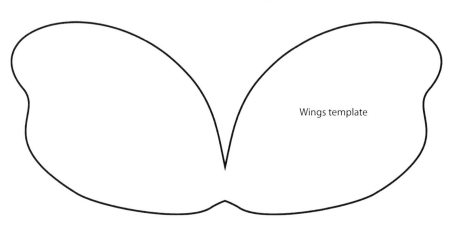

Wings template

13

Ready for the hot iron, Angelina fibres are sandwiched between two pieces of parchment

Turn on your iron and allow it to heat up to its maximum setting. Gently slide the template away from underneath the paper and then cover the Angelina fibres with the other half of the parchment. Place the hot iron on top of the paper with the Angelina fibre sandwiched between the two halves. Only run the iron across it for five to ten seconds. You will see that the colour of the Angelina fibres becomes more vibrant.

14

Open the parchment paper and your individual Angelina fibres will now have fused into a solid sheet. Lay the template underneath the sheet (it will still be see-through) as you did before the ironing. Use your waterproof pen to draw around the template underneath and cut out the wings.

You have two options for fastening them to the fairy's back: you can use wisps of the blue wool to needle felt them into place or you could glue them on. If you choose to use glue you will have to leave the glue to dry before continuing.

15

Finally, decorate your fairy to your liking with fabric flowers, gluing them into place. Either sit your fairy down or hang it up by a thread sewn through the top of the head.

Wind Sprite Fairy

I guess that the character of wind interpreted as a fairy would be different for different people depending on where in the world they live and depending on whether it is welcome or not. Personally, I imagine it to be tousled, delicate and a little elusive. This little sprite fits my imagination.

SKILL LEVEL
Crafty beginner
FINISHED SIZE
Size: 8–10cm (3¼–4in)
TECHNIQUES USED
Wrapping wire with wool, adding details

YOU WILL NEED

WOOL
2g (¹/₁₂oz) light-blue NZ Merino
1g (¹/₂₄oz) grey Gotland lamb batts
1g (¹/₂₄oz) pink Australian Merino batts
1g (¹/₂₄oz) white ramie top

EXTRAS
1 x 36cm (14¼in) length of #26 gauge paper-covered wire

TOOLS
#38 medium felting needle
#40 fine felting needle
#42 extra-fine felting needle
Felting mat
Wire cutters or old scissors
PVA glue

1

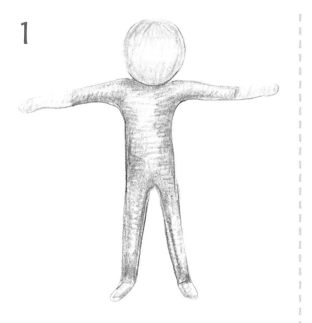

Follow the instructions for the Small Basic Fairy Body on page 20. When you get to the legs, cover the ends of the wire with pink – as you did for the hands, then cover the rest of the legs with light blue before fastening them to the body. Cover the body and upper arms with light blue too.

2

Take your grey Gotland wool and keep it flat, about 16 x 7cm (6¼ x 2¾in) in size, with the fibres running lengthways (it should fit into the open palm of your hand including fingers). Make a hole in the middle. Slip this over the fairy's head so that the long sides run down the front and back. Push the arms up, smooth the grey wool down with your hands and push it in on the sides.

3

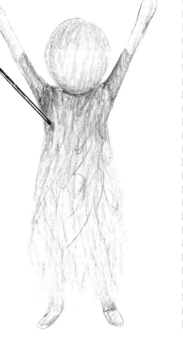

Felt the top part of the body down so that the grey wool is more shaped around the chest, neck and arms. Tear wispy ends off the base of the grey dress so that the feet and legs are visible. Do this by gently letting the fibres slither away. Hold on tight to the fairy's body so that you don't pull off her dress.

4

Hair

Take your white ramie tops – they should be no more than 20cm (8in) in length. Find the centre of the tops and lay this over the top of the head. These will be felted onto the fairy's head in one go starting on the front of the head. First, felt the white tops to the top of the head. The hair should look slightly dishevelled, so work your way around the head felting the hair on here and there. Make sure you felt the tops onto the head but leave the ends hanging down the back.

5

Eyes

Eyes are optional. If you do want to add eyes, use the light-blue wool to make tiny dots in the middle of the face.

Butterfly and Moth Fairy

The wings of these fairies are based on the Clifden Nonpareil moth (or Blue Underwing) and the Monarch butterfly – I chose the Blue Underwing and the Monarch because they are two of the largest butterflies and moths in the UK and they made the perfect wings for these tiny fairies.

YOU WILL NEED

Monarch butterfly girl

WOOL

2g (¹/₁₂oz) golden-orange NZ Merino batts

2g (¹/₁₂oz) pink Australian Merino batts

1g (¹/₂₄oz) orange-tone Australian Merino tops

1g (¹/₂₄oz) dyed-black NZ Merino

Wisps of white Australian Merino batts

EXTRAS

80cm (31½in) brown mohair yarn

36cm (14¼in) length of paper-covered #26 gauge wire

8 x 10cm (3⅛ x 4in) piece of water-soluble paper

50cm (19½in) strong thread

Blue Underwing moth boy

WOOL

2g (¹/₁₂oz) light-blue NZ Merino batts

2g (¹/₁₂oz) pink Australian Merino batts

1g (¹/₂₄oz) brown/grey South German Merino batts

Wisps of white Australian Merino batts and black NZ Merino batts

EXTRAS

80cm (31½in) white Little Loopy Locks

36cm (14¼in) length of paper-covered #26 gauge wire

8 x 10cm (3⅛ x 4in) piece of water-soluble paper

50cm (19½in) strong thread

TOOLS (for both)

#36 coarse felting needle

#38 medium felting needle

#40 fine felting needle

#42 extra-fine twisted felting needle

Sharp little scissors

Wire cutters or old scissors

Warm water and towel

Soft pencil

SKILL LEVEL
Crafty beginner

FINISHED SIZE
Moth:11cm (4¼in)
Butterfly: 9cm (3½in)

TECHNIQUES USED
Needle felting, wrapping
wool around wire,
adding details

1

Follow the instructions for the Small Basic Fairy Body on page 20. For the **butterfly fairy**, cover the body with the golden-orange wool batts.

For the **moth fairy**, add the legs 3cm (1¼in) below the head (instead of 2cm [¾in] for the butterfly) to make him taller. Cover him with light-blue wool batts.

2

Next for the **butterfly fairy**, take two strands of the orange tone tops, about 10cm (4in) long and no more than two fingers wide. Lay one strand underneath the fairy and one on top. Use your strong thread to tie the tops just underneath her arms and secure with a knot, making sure you have pulled it tight.

For the **moth fairy** you do not not need to add a top dress.

Pull the wispy ends that are above the tied waist down, front and back, so that they turn into a long skirt. Adjust with your fingers to close the sides. Use your scissors to trim the skirt so that the legs are visible all the way up to the orange tops covering the legs.

Hair

3

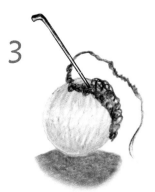

Take the brown mohair yarn and begin felting it onto the side of the **butterfly fairy's** head using your medium or fine felting needle. Frame the face first. Work your way around the whole of the head to give the fairy a full head of short hair.

For the **moth fairy** use the white Little Loopy Locks to cover the head in the same way as you did for the butterfly fairy.

4

Wings

Even though the butterfly and moth are fundamentally different their basic wing shapes are very similar, so use the same template for both. The wing size is close to life size with the **moth fairy** Blue Underwing's wingspan up to 9.5cm (3¾in) and the **butterfly fairy** Monarch's up to 10cm (4in). For both, start by tracing around the template on your water-soluble paper using a soft pencil.

5

Moth and butterfly wings template

Now it's time to colour in the shapes. It is important that you keep the wool cover thin but consistent with no bald patches. Use your coarse needle to start with and then go down to the medium or fine needle when adding details. You will have to lift your work off the mat regularly to stop it from fastening on and only stab from one side.

For the **Monarch butterfly fairy**, take a wisp of the golden-orange wool and lay it onto one of the top wings with loose fibres spilling over the edge. Initially, felt the fibres down in the middle, then trace the outline with your needle.

6

Tuck in any fibres that fall outside the felted line and felt down the inside of the shape. This should make a neat edge. Repeat for the other top wing. Make sure that the top wings overlap slightly into the bottom wings and that the two top wings have wool overlapping.

7

Colour in the bottom wings in the same way. Hold the paper up towards the light to check for thin patches and cover any you find with extra wisps of wool. Carefully add a border of black wool around the top of both wings, making it wider towards the tip (see above). From now on you need to work precisely and symmetrically: whatever you add on one side, needs to be added to the other side as exactly as you can manage.

8

Continue the black line of wool along the bottom of the top wings and fill the tips of the top wings in a little more.

Then add a black border around the bottom wing edges, taking care to keep the borders evenly wide.

9

Next, add the veins by felting a line from the corners of the top wings to the opposite sides. Add two smaller black lines branching off the main line.

Felt two curving lines on the bottom wings that meet one another halfway. Felt three more lines extending from the first two on the bottom wings and ending at the base of the bottom wings. Make any adjustments needed to ensure the wings are symmetrical.

10

Add two spots of orange wool to the tips of the top wings, on the black cover. Take a wisp of the white wool and roll it into a tiny ball between your fingers. Don't make it too tight as you may just stab it right through the wings; leave it a little fluffy. You will need to make around 40 tiny white dots of wool.

Add the first of the white dots below the orange spots on the tips of the top wings, then add a minimum of 10 white spots to the top wings along the black edge. When you add a dot to one wing, immediately add one to the same place on the other wing.

Do the same on the bottom wings, adding white dots to the black edges only. Aim for around nine white dots on each wing.

11

Once the butterfly is complete, cut off any excess water-soluble paper and neaten the edges. Dip your butterfly wings into a bowl of warm water for a couple of seconds. Squeeze the wings so that the water distributes evenly and the paper dissolves. The dissolving paper will make your fingers sticky and helps to stiffen the felted fabric.

Leave the wings to dry. Once the wings are dry, lay them onto your fairy's back facing up. Use your medium felting needle to stab into the centre of the butterfly wings and into the fairy's back. The wool in the wings should be enough to attach them but if it's not use a tiny amount of black wool in the centre of the wings to felt them on.

12

For the **moth fairy,** take the second template that you traced onto water-soluble paper and use the soft white wool batts to felt a border onto the outer edge (not the top edge) of the top wings. Use the same techniques you used for the butterfly wings to create a neat edge. Now create a border around the entire outline of the bottom wings.

13

Next, take the brown/grey wool batts and begin filling in the two top wings. Felt the wool in the middle first to secure it, then felt towards the edge, leaving about 2mm (1/8in) of the white border showing. The wool on the two top wings should overlap and the wool on the top wings should also overlap the bottom wings.

14

Mix some of the black wool with wisps of white (less white than black) to make a dark grey mix. Add this to the top of the bottom wings recreating their top lines.

Now add the light blue wool beneath the dark grey, keeping the edges soft. The blue can touch the white. Do this on both wings.

Add the dark grey mix below the light blue. The stripes should be curved and come up to meet the tops of the bottom wings.

15

Check that there are no thin patches by holding the moth up to the light. Add wisps of wool to fill any weak spots, always overlapping with the existing wool layer.

Cut around the shape, taking off any excess paper and neatening the edges. Dissolve the paper and leave to dry as you did before.

Finally, felt the moth wings onto the back of the fairy in the same way as you did for the butterfly.

Sun Fairy

The sun fairy represents many aspects of nature.
I see her less as a fiery symbol and more as a
source of energy, gently warming the air and
breathing life into nature. She can also be a
sunflower fairy!

YOU WILL NEED
WOOL
5g (¹⁄₆oz) standard core batts

South American Merino tops:

    6g (¹⁄₅oz) dyed yellow

    6g (¹⁄₅oz) natural dark brown

3g (¹⁄₈oz) orange Mountain sheep batts

3g (¹⁄₈oz) brown-dyed curls

20cm (8in) length of yellow bamboo fibre

EXTRAS
1 x 30cm (12in) extra-strong pipe cleaner

50cm (19¾in) strong brown thread

50cm (19¾in) silky thread

TOOLS
#38 medium felting needle

Sewing needle

PVA glue

Pliers

Scissors

Felting mat (optional)

Wire cutters or old scissors

PVA glue

SKILL LEVEL
Crafty beginner
FINISHED SIZE
20cm (8in) long
TECHNIQUES USED
Wire wrapping and a little
needle felting

1

Make a basic fairy shape by following the Large Basic Fairy Body instructions on page 16, but use the dark-brown tops for the head and arms, and brown thread to tie it in place. In Step 4 (page 18) you should use a 16–18cm (6¼–7in) length of pipe cleaner, so use the second pipe cleaner to cut to size.

2

Take the orange Mountain sheep batts and flatten them out into a shape about the size of the inside of the flat of your hand. This piece should not be too thick, so remove some layers if necessary. Make a hole in the centre and slip it over the fairy's head so that the longer sides run down the front and back of the body.

Make sure that the side of the head with the smoothest brown covering faces forwards. Gently felt down the orange batts that cover the upper body and slip those that lie over the arms as far up the upper arms as possible.

3

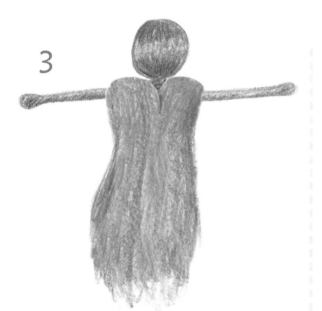

Next take the dyed yellow wool tops and gently tear off two equal lengths of about 10cm (4in). Put these aside to use for the wings later. The remaining yellow tops will be used for the top layer of the fairy's dress. Make a hole in the centre to fit over her head. Place the yellow tops over the head and smooth them down over her body.

4

Felt the upper half of the body gently with your felting needle so that the arms remain free, and the high waist is slightly tucked in. Next, take the yellow bamboo fibre and tie it around her waist. Make sure that the top half of the fairy looks even and that the upper arm cover is slightly puffy, but not too loose.

5

Hair

The fairy's hair is intended to look like a bob hairstyle, so you will have to cut the brown-dyed curls shorter and/or cut them to separate them out. Start by framing the face with the curls. Gently stab the first small batch of them onto the side of the face. Make sure that you keep as much texture as you can in the curls and don't flatten them. Using small batches, work your way around the front part of the fairy's head first, then turn the fairy over and cover the back of the head.

6

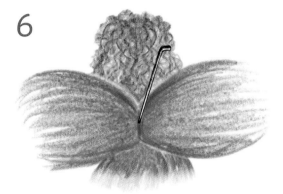

Wings

To make the wings, use the two lengths of the dyed yellow wool tops and put them on top of one another to make a thick single layer. Felt this layer onto the back of the fairy, below the head, stabbing only along the centre of the wings. You will find that if you concentrate on one area rather than a line, the centre will pull together, and the wings will look as though they are pinched in the middle.

7

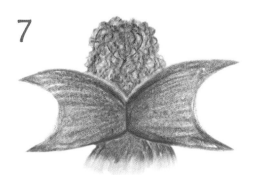

Once the wings are fastened on, split each wing into two by gently separating the fibres. Then twist the ends of the fibres into little points with your fingers.

Separate the bottom front of the dress into three parts and twist the ends, just as you did for the wings. Repeat the same process on the back of the fairy's dress.

It is OK for a little orange wool to show but you should make sure that the dress is widened at the bottom; manipulate it with your fingers only – no needle felting is required.

Water

Water Nymph

Imagine a hot summer's day and how busy it gets around a pond. That's where you might find a water nymph dancing on the glistening surface of the water – if you look carefully!

SKILL LEVEL
Crafty beginner
FINISHED SIZE
14cm (5¾in)
TECHNIQUES USED
Wrapping wool around wire, adding features

YOU WILL NEED

WOOL
1g (¹/₂₄oz) waterfall Merino/silk mix batts
1g (¹/₂₄oz) blue/turquoise tone wool tops
1g (¹/₂₄oz) pink Australian Merino batts
Tiny wisps of medium-blue and flamingo-pink for eyes and a mouth (optional)

EXTRAS
1 x 36cm (14in) length of #26 gauge paper-covered wire
1g (¹/₂₄oz) mermaid hand-dyed Teeswater curls
30cm (12in) strong thread
2 x pairs of organza dragonfly wings

TOOLS
#38 medium felting needle
#40 fine felting needle
#42 extra-fine felting needle
Felting mat
PVA glue
Wire cutters or old scissors to cut wire

1

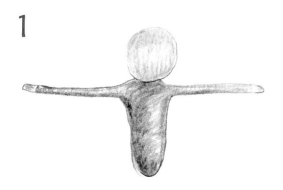

Follow the instructions for the Small Basic Fairy Body on page 20. Use the pink wool for the hands and the waterfall batts for the arms. This fairy has no legs, but cover the whole body with the waterfall batts.

2

Next, take the blue/turquoise tops – about 20cm (8in) long – and make a hole in the centre. Slip the tops over the fairy's head and push the arms up to stop the tops from slipping off. Smooth the fibres down with your hands then tie a high waistline with your strong thread.

3

Wings

Cross the two pairs of organza dragonfly wings over in the centre and lay them onto the back of the fairy, adjust their position and felt them down in the centre of the back with a tiny amount of the waterfall wool.

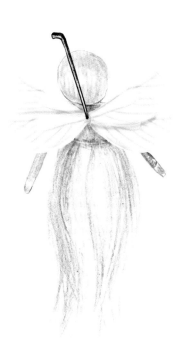

4

Hair

Cut shorter strands from the Teeswater curls and and/or separate them using scissors (don't pull them apart, that makes them frizzy). Use your medium felting needle to felt one curl strand onto the side of the head framing one side of the face, then felt a curl onto the other side of the fairy's face. Now cover the back of the head too.

5

Eyes and mouth

Using your fine needle, felt tiny eyes with the medium blue – you could make closed-looking eyes by felting a thin strand of wool into a curve. Then make the mouth using the flamingo-pink wool. Neaten the base of the dress by gently pulling off strands of the wool – this will give it a fresh, wispy look.

Ice Fairy

Cool, graceful, majestic and powerful, yet so vulnerable too! She reminds me of the fragility of the Antarctic ice sheet and how none of us ever imagined that one day it could be gone! A cruel reminder of global warming.

YOU WILL NEED

WOOL
5g (¹/₆oz) cream standard core batts
5g (¹/₆oz) white Shetland batts (in one flat sheet)
6g (¹/₅oz) pink South American Merino tops
7g (¹/₄oz) white extra-fine Merino tops
4g (¹/₇oz) short, extra-white Teeswater curls

EXTRAS
1 x 30cm (12in) extra-strong pipe cleaner
1m (39½in) of extra-strong thread
50cm (19¾in) of silky thread
1 pair of wings
1 rose-gold crown
3 x snowflakes
3 x silver stars
1 x 25cm (10in) length of sequins or beads

TOOLS
#38 medium felting needle
Sewing needle
PVA glue
Pliers
Scissors
Felting mat (optional)

SKILL LEVEL
Crafty beginner
FINISHED SIZE
16–17cm (6¼–6¾in) long
TECHNIQUES USED
Wire wrapping and a
little needle felting

1

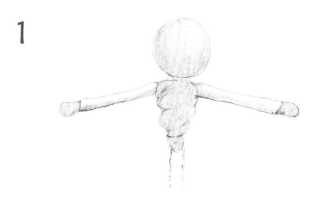

Make a base shape according to the Large Basic Fairy Body instructions on page 16. Note that in Step 4 (page 18) you should use a 16–18cm (6¼–7in) length of pipe cleaner, which you take from the main pipe cleaner once the head is done.

Use the white wool tops to make the arms (NOT the white Shetland batts). Take care not to mess up the tops as they are also used for the smooth main dress – just gently separate a thin strand running along the length.

2

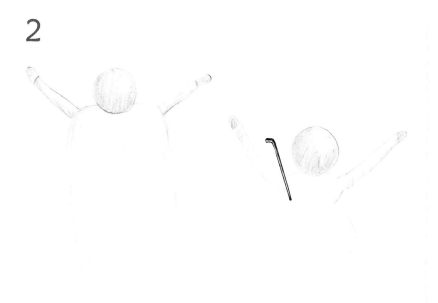

3

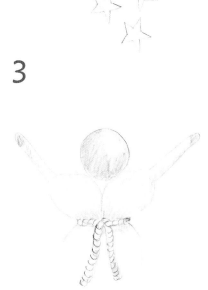

Take the white Shetland batts – they look like a lofty sheet rather than a long strand of fine wool – and flatten the sheet out to approximately 10 x 20cm (4 x 8in). Make a hole in the centre. Bend the arms down first then slip the batts over the fairy's head, so that the long sides are at the front and back.

Bend the arms up, which helps to hold the wool in place and, with your felting needle, gently stab the wool down on the top part of the fairy to reveal her arms again.

Take the strand of fine white wool tops and, once again, make a hole in the centre, then slip it over the fairy as you did before. Take the length of sequin or bead trim and tie it around the fairy's waist, just beneath the arms. Pull it tight and secure it with a knot. Make sure that the wool on the arms looks the same on each side.

4

Wings

Use a generous dab of glue to attach the wings onto the back of the fairy, then leave it to dry. If you are impatient, you can use a glue gun, superglue or any other clear-drying glue.

5

Hair

Sort through the extra white Teeswater curls and, if you need to separate them, use scissors rather than tearing them. Start by felting a couple of curly strands onto each side of the head to frame the face, then work your way around the head. You may have enough curls left to add another layer. If you tease the curls sideways at the top, they are easier to felt on.

Glue the little crown onto the fairy's head.

6

Have your glue at the ready to decorate the fairy to your liking with the snowflakes and the little silver stars. To hang the fairy, insert thread through the centre of the crown, either before you glue it on or once the glue has dried. Keep a little of the silky thread aside to hang the bell, which the fairy can hold in her hand.

Water Fairy

Water is a powerful element, one capable of both giving and taking life. A reminder that, as humans, we are at the mercy of Mother Nature.

SKILL LEVEL
Crafty beginner

FINISHED SIZE
18cm (7in) long

TECHNIQUES USED
Wire wrapping and a little needle felting

YOU WILL NEED

WOOL
5g (1/6oz) standard core/stuffing batts
5g (1/6oz) pink South American Merino tops
4g (1/7oz) royal-blue NZ Merino batts
5g (1/6oz) midnight-blue Rainbow Drops NZ Merino batts
3g (1/8oz) turquoise-blue tones Australian Merino tops

For the wings
2g (1/12oz) of white seashell shimmer NZ Merino batts
Wisp of aquamarine Mountain sheep batts
Wisp of white Seacell fibre

EXTRAS
1 x 30cm (12in) extra-strong pipe cleaner
50cm (19¾in) of extra-strong thread
30cm (12in) of sparkly thread
18cm (7in) of pearl trim
1 piece of sea glass
6–8 seashell sequins
10 x small light-blue rhinestones
2 x large light-blue rhinestones
2 x white acrylic crystals
5 x water drop shaped decorations

TOOLS
#38 medium felting needle
Sewing needle
PVA glue
30 x 60cm (12 x 24in) bubble wrap
Warm water
Soap (hand soap or washing up liquid)
Towel

1

Make a base shape according to the Large Basic Fairy Body instructions on page 16. The diameter of the head should be 3.5–4cm (1¼–1½in). In Step 4 (page 18) you should use a 16–18cm (6¼–7in) length of pipe cleaner, which you take from the main pipe cleaner once the head is done. Use the pink wool top to make the hands and arms.

2

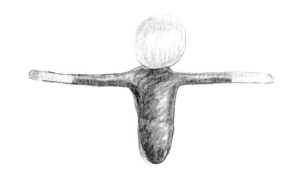

Take a wisp of the royal-blue tops (the lighter blue without the colourful spots) and start dressing the upper body of the fairy by wrapping the wool in thin, flat layers around the upper arms and body. Work with small batches of wool and keep the layers thin.

Use many thin layers to build up bulk and coverage. Cover the whole upper body and bend the pipe cleaner end in too. Felt any wispy ends down as and when needed. The upper body should be 3.5–4cm (1¼–1½in) wide if measured under the arms.

3

Split the midnight blue wool into two flat batches – each one large enough to cover half of your open hand from mid palm to the ends of fingers. Lay one half onto the back of the fairy and the other half onto the front so that it goes just over the fairy's waist.

Use your felting needle and felt the waist area down so that you create a flat area before the unfelted wool hangs down from the waist. Tie the pearl trim around the waist. You may have to use a wisp of the midnight-blue wool to felt into the tied front to secure it.

4

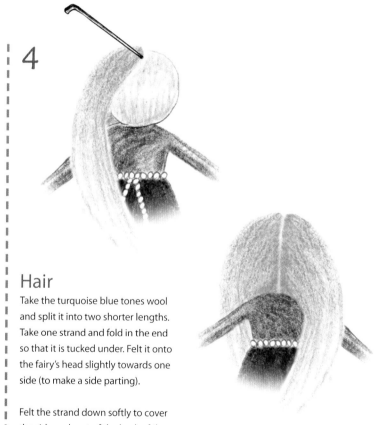

Hair

Take the turquoise blue tones wool and split it into two shorter lengths. Take one strand and fold in the end so that it is tucked under. Felt it onto the fairy's head slightly towards one side (to make a side parting).

Felt the strand down softly to cover the side and part of the back of the head. Repeat this process on the other side of the head, meeting the folded edge with the second folded strand.

Again, felt down softly on the side and back of the head. The two strands should be split at the back where they hang down.

5

Wings

Prepare a small bowl of warm water and add either a tiny drop of liquid soap or submerge a soap bar in it and move it around so the water becomes soapy. You only need very little soap, just enough to build a lather when felting the wool. The wings will not be fully felted but will have a lacy finish.

6

Take wisps of the white seashell shimmer and lay them out on your bubble wrap (bubbles facing up) so that the fibres run sideways/horizontally. Then take the aquamarine wool and lay wisps of it over the top of the white seashell shimmer wisps. On top of those, add wisps of the white Seacell fibres. Add drops of soapy water so that the wool is thoroughly wet.

7

Fold the bubble wrap over and rub the top of it with the wet woolly wings inside. You will have to do this rigorously so that the fibres start to felt together. It helps if the top of the bubble wrap is slippery. Check if the wool is holding together and, if not, repeat the process. You can also felt the wool further by just using your fingers and soapy water. Rub the areas you want to felt. Once the wings are lightly felted, rinse the soap out altogether and leave them to dry. You can trim the wings later if needed.

8

Once the wings are totally dry, pinch them in the middle and felt the middle down onto the fairy's upper back. You may need to use an extra wisp of wool. Make sure that the prettier side of the wings points forwards. Once they are secure, decorate the wings with the small, light-blue rhinestones by gluing them on. Use only a small amount of glue so that you do not add extra weight. Leave to dry.

9

To decorate the fairy further you could glue the little blue seashells onto the hair, glue the water drop shaped decorations onto the front of the dress and the larger rhinestone and acrylic crystals to the base of the dress. To make a hanging fairy, sew a loop of thread onto the top of the fairy's head.

Kingfisher

On the few occasions I have spotted a kingfisher when walking beside streams, I have felt incredibly happy and, frankly, it made my day. Usually, I only get a glimpse of the flashing, electric blue colours before I blink, and the little bird has disappeared. I love these birds for the yellow-orange colours that clash with the vibrant blues – opposites on the colour wheel, yet perfectly paired in nature.

SKILL LEVEL
Beginner to advanced

FINISHED SIZE
16cm (6¼in) from the tail to the top of head

TECHNIQUES USED
3- and 2-D shaping, attaching shapes and features

YOU WILL NEED

WOOL BATTS
20g (²/₃oz) cream luxury organic core wool
3g (¹/₈oz) blue/green shimmer
3g (¹/₈oz) royal-blue NZ Merino
3g (¹/₈oz) golden-orange NZ Merino
3g (¹/₈oz) MS aqua
3g (¹/₈oz) white Cape Merino
1g (¹/₂₄oz) black NZ Merino

EXTRAS
Small, white wire bird legs
7mm black glue-in eyes
Orange florist tape
Water
2 x 5 x 10cm (2 x 4in) pieces of soluble paper

TOOLS
#38 medium felting needle
#36 coarse felting needle
#40 fine felting needle
Felting mat
Soft pencil
Sharp little scissors
PVA glue

1

Body

Take half of the cream core wool for the body (10g [⅓oz]) and split it into one third and two thirds quantities. Use the larger two thirds amount and fold it in on itself into an oval shape. Felt it down so that it holds its shape. Take the remaining one third and wrap around the shape to make it slightly longer at one end. Using your coarse needle felt it down so that the shape measures about 10 x 5cm (4 x 2in). Put this aside while you start making the head.

2

Beak and head

Take about one third of the remaining white wool (3g [⅛oz]) and flatten it into a sheet measuring 22 x 10cm (8¾ x 4in). Fold in half widthways (it should be almost square now). Roll the folded front in really tightly – this will be the beak and should be about 4cm (1½in) long. Felt just that pointy part down well and keep the rest of the shape unfelted. The beak needs to be solidly felted so go down to a medium or even fine needle to firm it up.

3

Next, use a pinch of the cream wool to make an egg shape (a miniature version of the body) that is about 4 x 2cm (1½ x ¾in) in size. Insert it into the head part, which is unfelted, so that it sits in there horizontal to the head. Stab into the head and the egg shape to secure it.

4

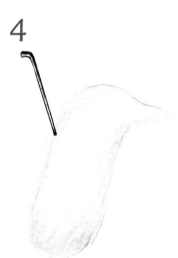

Spread the loose head fibres of the head with beak out over the body so that the beak is at a right angle to the upright oblong body. Pull the fibres down and felt them while holding them taut. Felt all around to fasten the head to the body part securely.

5

Take some of the remaining cream wool and layer three or four batches on top of one another to make a wad of wool. Lay this wad onto the bird's tummy. Felt it down by stabbing into the edges of the wad first before reducing the size by stabbing into it too. This should add bulk to the kingfisher's tummy and make it rounder.

6

Take wisps of the royal blue and black wools and mix them together to make a dark midnight-blue colour. Do this by laying the fibres on top of one another, then teasing them apart with your fingers until you have an even mix. Lay the new colour thinly onto the beak and felt it down. You may have to add more to cover bare patches.

Cover the underside of the beak with the golden orange wool, following the shape of the beak but still showing dark blue on the side and towards the tip of the beak.

7

Next, cover the head with the white Cape Merino wool. You may have to use your fine felting needle for this.

Then, mix the blue/green shimmer and the royal-blue wool to create a new mix and lay it over the top of the head, starting from the front and working towards the back of the head. Felt it down. It should be like a little cap on top of the head. Make sure it is symmetrical. This is also a good time to flatten the kingfisher's head.

8

Use the same mix, but a little darker, to make a stripe at the side of the head starting from the centre of the beak and reaching back towards the neck. Repeat on the other side. Keep checking for symmetry by looking at the bird's face straight on.

Then, cover the gap between the cap and the stripe with golden orange.

9

10

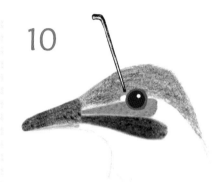

Eyes

Take your coarse felting needle and insert it into the side of the head on the line of the golden orange and the cap, about 1.5cm (½in) away from where the beak starts. Push it all the way in until the fatter part of the needle is inserted. This will

make a hole for the eye. Insert the pin of the eye. Repeat on the other side. If the eyes are symmetrical, put a dab of glue behind each eye – without taking them out – push them back in and leave them to dry.

Use the white Cape Merino and the black NZ wool to mix a dark grey. Twist a wisp between your fingers to make a thin strand. Felt the strand around the eye to make an eyelid. Repeat on the other side.

Next, add a tiny white and golden-orange spot (orange above the white) in front of the eye. Repeat on the other side.

11

Tail

Take a pinch of the cream core wool and keep it flat. You need a piece about 5 x 6cm (2 x 2½in). Felt one end into a blunt triangular shape by folding the wool inwards and stabbing down. Leave the end, about 2cm (¾in), unfelted. Work the tail tip from both sides, then open out the unfelted wisps so that they can fit onto the end of the kingfisher.

12

When you place the tail next to the body it may appear large, but once fitted it will shrink in size. Fit the loose ends of the tail around the tip of the body and then felt it down with your coarse felting needle. Reduce the size, if needed, by felting into the tail towards the body at a shallow angle.

13

Body and tail viewed from above

Use the golden orange to cover the whole of the underside of the bird in a thin layer from the neck all the way down to the underside of the tail.

Use the aqua and blue/green shimmer wools to make up a new wool mix; keep the colour light by using more aqua. Lay this onto the back of the bird in the direction that the feathers would run and felt it down. Cover the whole of the bird's back including the back of the tail. Work symmetrically.

14

Add a covering of white Cape Merino to the side of the bird between the orange and blue.

Use the darker blue/green shimmer and royal blue mix to add a small wedge on the side of the tail.

15

Wings

Take one of the sheets of water-soluble paper and, using the template (right), draw around the outline for one wing. Make a small batch of the blue/green shimmer and royal blue mix in the same shade as used for the top of the head. Lay the mix thinly onto the water-soluble paper and felt it down in the middle of the shape by stabbing into it with your coarse felting needle. Lift it off the mat, then trace the outer line with your needle before folding the fibres outside the line inwards. Felt these down.

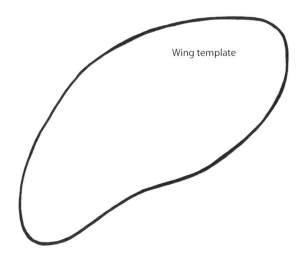

Wing template

16

1. Keep lifting the paper off your felting mat. Felt all over to neaten it, but only felt from the top/one side. Use your scissors to cut off the excess paper.

2. Add a dusting of the aqua and blue/green shimmer mix by laying down wisps at the narrower end of the wing. Felt them down with your medium felting needle.

3. Then add a tiny amount of the royal blue/black mix you used for the beak to the tip of the wing. Mix a little of the blue mix and the dark blue mix together, then felt it over the join to soften it. Make a second wing in the same way.

17

Felt the wing onto the side of the kingfisher so that the rounded wing corresponds with the roundness of the tummy. Felt the top on too but check from above that the two wings are even.

18

Use the light mix (the same one you used on the back and on the tips of the wings) to add a dusting to the front top of the head. Keep it very thin. Your kingfisher is ready to receive his legs.

19

Legs and feet

Take the small white wire legs and tear off a short strip of the orange florist tape. Florist tape (see above) becomes sticky when stretched. Wrap the legs with the orange tape, working with small lengths and remembering to stretch the tape so that it sticks. Wrap the tape only up half of the vertical leg 'stalks'. Leaving the top bare helps to fasten the legs into the bird. Cover all the toes but leave the very ends uncovered (white). If you like you can colour these in with a water proof pen to be black. Otherwise leave white. Once you've wrapped the fourth claw at the back leave the rest of the bend uncovered. This bend helps to make the legs more stable when fastening into the bird and stops the legs from swivelling whilst waiting for the glue to dry.

20

Bend the top of the legs in towards the toes at an angle. Make holes into the tummy of the kingfisher so that they will follow the bent line of the wire legs. Insert the legs so that only 1cm (3/8in) of leg shows. Fasten them in by using glue and leaving it to dry. Once the glue is dry, felt wisps of golden orange over the holes to cover where the legs are secured. You can bend the three front toes to look more realistic, and also cut the wire join between the feet if you like.

Frog

I love frogs and one was always going to be a part of this book. In fact, I surprised myself with how easily the design ran off my fingers. It may have something to do with the fact that as a child I spent hours looking at them while trying to catch them (and let them go again of course). Even as an adult I am always up for holding a frog like others might want to hold a puppy. This frog is the rare Northern Pool Frog, only found in the Breckland District in East Anglia in the UK. This one is larger than life size and could be used as a basic model for other frogs or toads.

YOU WILL NEED

WOOL BATTS
15g (½oz) cream lanolin-rich core wool
10g (⅓oz) beige Karakul Merino
2g (¹/₁₂oz) olive-green Australian Merino
1g (¹/₂₄oz) brown Portuguese Merino
1g (¹/₂₄oz) light-yellow NZ Merino

EXTRAS
5mm black glue-in eyes
4 x 36cm (14¼in) lengths of #26 gauge paper-covered wire
3 x 36cm (14¼in) lengths of #22 gauge paper-covered wire
Reel of beige 5mm florist tape

TOOLS
#38 medium felting needle
#36 coarse felting needle
Felting mat
PVA glue
Wire cutters

SKILL LEVEL
Crafty beginner to advanced

FINISHED SIZE
12cm (4¾in) long with legs tucked under

TECHNIQUES USED
Wire wrapping with florist tape and wool, shaping and attaching features

1

Legs and feet

Prepare your four lengths of #26 gauge wire by cutting them into 16 shorter lengths of 9cm (3½in). Wrap them with florist tape, folding one end in and covering the bend in florist tape too. You need four covered lengths for each foot.

2 Front legs toes

Cut your thicker #22 gauge wires into halves. Use one wire for each foot and fold it around the toes to trap them.

For the HIND LEGS work it so that you have toes 1 and 3 at 4cm (1½in), toe 2 (middle) at 5cm (2in) and toe 4 at 3cm (1¼in).

For the FRONT LEGS you need the toes to measure as follows: toe 1 and 2 at 2cm (¾in) and toes 3 and 4 at 3cm (1¼in).

3

Front legs

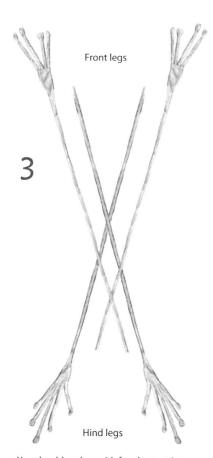

Hind legs

You should end up with four legs – wire from the ankle to the end measuring about 16cm (6¼in). Cover the remaining wire with the beige florist tape.

Front legs

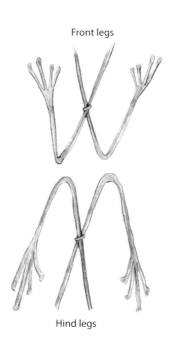

Hind legs

Then bend the leg ends as follows:
FRONT LEGS – bend at 3cm (1¼in) from ankle to elbow. Cross the leg at a 3cm (1¼in) mark.
HIND LEGS – bend at 5cm (2in) from ankle to knee. Cross the leg at 4cm (1½in) mark. Twist the crossing wires once to keep them in place. You could also add a little more florist tape to on top to secure them.

4

Body wire

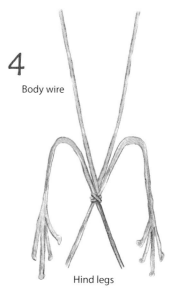

Hind legs

Take the remaining #22 gauge wire and cover it with florist tape. The wire will need to connect the front and back legs by hooking into the hind leg crossover and going back to the front leg crossover.

First, fold the main body wire in half and twist the wire around the hind leg crossover so that the wire faces up towards the front legs.

5

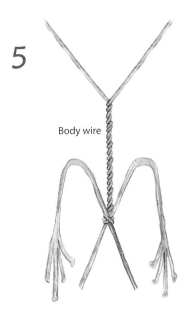
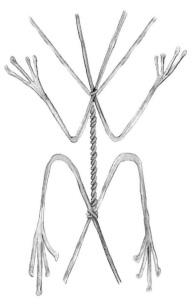

Body wire

Twist the main body wire around itself for about 6cm (2¼in) to make the body length.

Trap the front legs at the crossover as you did with the hind legs.

6

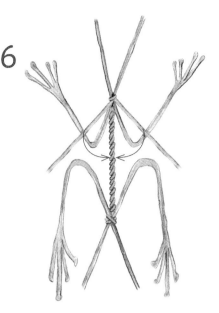

Then wrap the main body wire back around the central body (see arrows above). Cut it short if it extends the body. This will have strengthened the body. You still have two wires sticking out at each end of the frog. The front wires will become the head.

7

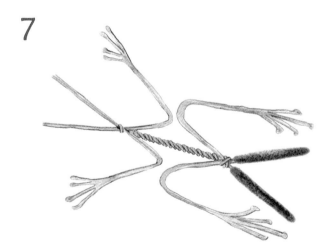

The back wires become the ridges on the frog's back. Cover these lengths with the olive-green wool. When wrapping wire with wool, work with small wispy strands, wrap the wool flat like a ribbon and work close to the wire. Once they are covered with wool, bend the ends in and go over the bend again to secure it. Do this on both wires, making sure that you have enough length left to fit over the back of the frog.

8

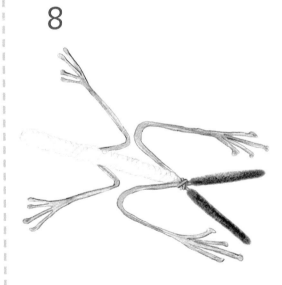

On the opposite end wrap the two head wire lengths with the cream core wool. Again, bend the ends in as close to the end as possible. Add another thin layer to secure. Continue wrapping the head and the body with the same cream core wool. The lanolin-rich wool is perfect for wrapping wire because it almost sticks to itself. Keep the tension high and make a dense wrap.

9

Continue adding layers of core wool until your frog's body measures about 5–6cm (2–2¼in) in diameter. If you keep the wraps tight you will not need to use your felting needle yet; however, you can felt loose ends in with the needle if you need to. The head needs to be a little thinner than the body and tapered towards the front.

10

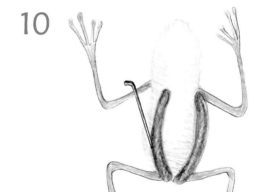

Bend the green-covered wires upwards. Use your felting needle to felt the wire ridges down onto the body, slightly curving outwards. Stab your medium felting needle into the green wool continuing into the cream body. Take care that your needle does not hit the wire.

11

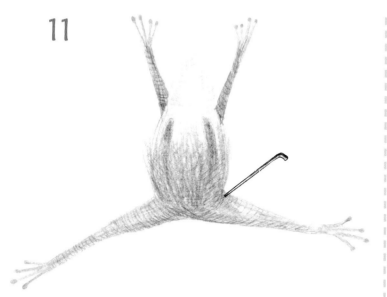

Take the beige wool and wrap the legs starting at the foot end. Build up more bulk towards the top/thigh end of the leg. Felt the wool down if needed and add more layers until the upper legs are about 2cm (¾in) thick and the lower legs 1cm (³⁄₈in) thick. Use the same wool to cover the very back of the frog, building up a little bulk at the same time and working your way along the top of the frog.

12

Bend the hind legs in so that they are tucked underneath the body. Do the same with the front legs. This position will now be the permanent pose.

13

Add the beige covering all over, including on the sides, ridges and head of the frog. Then use the olive green to cover two stripes between the ridges, keeping a line of beige in the middle. The cover should have a mottled appearance so that it looks more natural.

Cover the top of the head with the olive-green wool too.

14

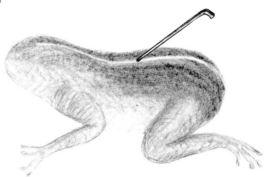

Mix the light-yellow and the cream core wool to make a more natural yellow mix and add it to the side of the frog, as well as the middle line, taking it all the way from the back to the top of the head.

15

16

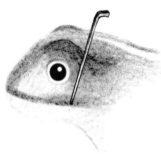

Eyes

Use the cream core wool to felt a disc shape onto the side of the head on each side, keeping the discs symmetrical. Use your felting needle to make a hole by inserting the needle as far as you can into the thicker part of the head. Take the needle out and insert the glue-in eye. Repeat on the other side. When the eyes are correctly positioned, add a dab of glue behind them without taking them out, push them back in and leave to dry.

You now need to build up the domed shape of the eye. Take a small amount of beige wool and shape it in your fingers to resemble a small bean. Felt this onto the top of where the eye is. Repeat on the other side and then cover the top again with olive green. If the domed shape is not large enough, add more beige before covering it with olive green wool again.

Northern Pool frogs have a green line running from the front of the frog's face, slightly above where you expect the mouth to be, and along their sides. Add a few green patches onto the side of the frog to break up the beige cover.

Minnow Fish

Not everything in nature has to be bright, big and rare! Every little creature has a purpose – we must never forget that!

SKILL LEVEL
Crafty beginner
FINISHED SIZE
10cm (4in) long
TECHNIQUES USED
Water-soluble paper, adding features

YOU WILL NEED

WOOL BATTS
2g (1/12oz) white Cape Merino
Wisp of natural-black Stone sheep lamb
Wisp of natural-orange NZ Merino
Wisp of olive-green Australian Merino

EXTRAS
Wisp of Angelina fibre
12 x 5cm (4¾ x 2in) piece of water-soluble paper

TOOLS
#38 medium felting needle
Felting mat
Soft pencil
Scissors
Bowl of warm water and a towel

1

Use your soft pencil to draw around the template (see below) of the fish outline onto the water-soluble paper. Use your white felting wool and medium felting needle to begin filling in the inside of the fish.

Turn the paper over and add a thin layer on the other side as well.

Minnow template

2

Cover the fins with thin wisps of white wool, making sure that the wool overlaps the main body. Felt the body and the fins from both sides. Cut the shape out neatening the edges. The white should so far only be a thin cover.

3

Now add more layers to the fish body (not the fins and tail) to make the fish more rounded. You will have to add a few wisps of wool over the top and bottom to cover where the water-soluble paper may be visible. Your fish should now be nice and round.

4

Mix a small amount of natural black and white wool with just a tiny amount of Angelina fibre. Mix the wool fibres by laying them on top of one another, teasing them apart with your thumb and index finger and repeating the process until the grey mix has a sparkling effect. Add a thin layer of the mix onto both sides of the fish.

Then add a tiny amount – like a dusting – of the natural-orange wool too.

5

Take a tiny amount of natural black and twist it between your fingers into a thin strand. Felt it down in a curve where the tail starts. Repeat on the other side. Take a similar amount of black and felt it onto the head to form a large black eye. Repeat on the other side.

6

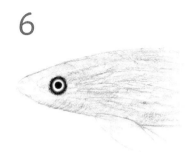

Eyes

Take a smaller amount of white wool and felt a smaller disc onto the black wool disc. Then add an even smaller black spot onto the white. Using your grey wool mix, shape a small strand between your fingers that you can felt down around the black disc with the white disc in the centre. Make both sides of the fish the same.

7

Use the natural-black wool to add a curved line where the head starts (as you did with the tail) as well as a horizontal line going along the centre of the body. Add a little natural orange onto the side of the face. Repeat on the other side.

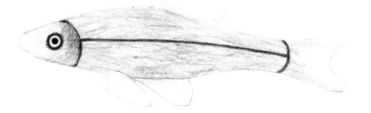

8

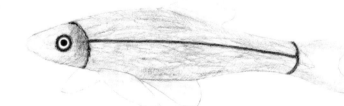

Mirror the front fin on the other side of the fish by using a wisp of natural wool. Attach with your felting needle. These fins at the front, underneath the fish, should be positioned against the side of the body. Use your felting needle to manipulate them with your needle to make them lie along the body.

OPTIONAL: You can rinse the water-soluble paper out of the tail and fins by dipping just these parts into the bowl of warm water. Dab them dry with a towel and leave them to dry.

Dragonfly Fairy

If you are not already fascinated by dragonflies for their colours, size and helicopter-like flying style, surely you will be when you find out that they were one of the first winged insects to evolve more than 300 million years ago. Did you know that they starve if they cannot fly as they can only eat in mid-air? In some cultures, dragonflies mean good luck. I love these insects!

SKILL LEVEL
Crafty beginner

FINISHED SIZE
10cm (4in) long

TECHNIQUES USED
Wrapping wire with wool
on a miniature scale

YOU WILL NEED

WOOL
Pinch of pink Australian Merino
Pinch of berries space-dyed wool top
1g (1/24oz) waterfall Merino/silk batts

EXTRAS
1x 36cm (14¼in) length of #26 gauge
paper-covered wire
Black or dark brown florist tape
2 x sets of organza dragonfly wings

TOOLS
#40 fine felting needle
Felting mat
Scissors
PVA glue

1

Cut your paper-covered wire as follows: 1 x 12cm (4¾in) length and 3 x 8cm (3⅛in) lengths. Take the longest length and insert the end about 2–3cm (¾–1¼in) into the nozzle of the glue bottle to add a tiny bit of glue. Then take a wisp of the pink wool and begin wrapping the end, allowing the glue to grip the wool. Cover the end thinly for about 2cm (¾in).

2

Bend the covered end of the wire in by about 1cm (³⁄₈in) so that the wool is trapped. Build more layers by wrapping the wool thinly and flat like a ribbon around the wire. Use your fine needle to felt the ball shape down, then add more layers. Make sure to felt into the base of the ball shape to keep it round. You are aiming for a ball shape of a finished size of 1.5cm (⁵⁄₈in).

3

Take one of the shorter wire lengths and about 7cm (2¾in), of the black or brown florist tape. Begin wrapping the tape around one end of the wire. Note that florist tape needs to be stretched to become sticky. Alternatively, you could use black wool to wrap the wire. Bend the end of the wire in by no more than 0.5cm (²⁄₈in). Cover the bend and continue along the wire. Make sure you stretch the tape and that it overlaps by more than half.

4

Stop at the middle of the wire and then cover the other end in the same way. It helps to always wrap the tape in the same direction, especially when starting at the opposite end. Use the warmth of your fingers to smooth the tape – twist the covered wire between your fingers if the tape is loose. Repeat this process on the other two short wire lengths.

5

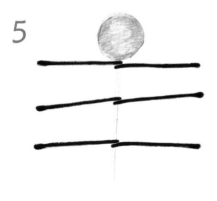

Next, take the three covered wires and wrap them once around the main body wire (white). Space them out at 1.5cm (⁵⁄₈in) intervals. You should end up with a tail end of about 6cm (2¼in). Do not wrap the white body wire around the legs (covered wire).

6

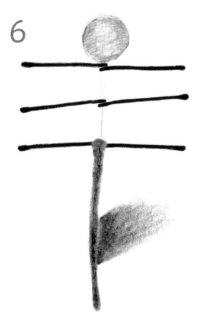

Dip the end of the white body wire into the nozzle of your glue for 2cm (¾in) and use the waterfall wool batts to start wrapping the wire end. Keep the wool flat and thin again. Then bend the end in by 0.5cm (²⁄₈in) and cover the bent end, keeping the cover thin. Continue wrapping the tail end until you get to the first set of legs. Wrap the wool around the leg/wire connections.

7

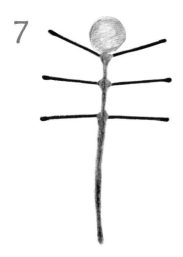

Take a new wisp of the waterfall wool and wrap around the same leg connection again, then work your way up towards the middle leg set. Wrap the wool around the connection there and finally the top set of legs. Bend the legs up or down as required so that they do not get in the way.

8

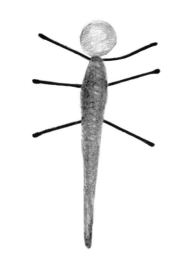

Now start at the tail end again repeating the whole process but this time making sure that the cover is neat and tight as it will be the final cover. Felt down as required. The tapered tail will be about 0.5cm (^{2}/$_8$in) going up to 1cm (^{3}/$_8$in) towards the body. Always wrap the wool in the same direction, especially when you start with a new strand. Add neat wraps over the body and between the legs and build up bulk.

9

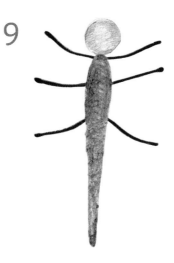

Once you have finished the body wrap, take a thin strand of the pink wool top (berries), about 15cm (6in) and establish it at the tail end. Then wrap upwards, creating a candy-stripe effect, and finish just under the first set of legs. Felt down as needed.

10

Face
Take two tiny wisps of the waterfall wool and felt two eyes onto the middle line of the face. Take a similar size tiny wisp from the berries top to felt a little mouth below.

11

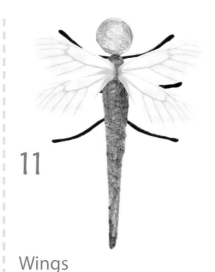

Wings
Take two sets of organza dragonfly wings and position them on the back of the dragonfly between the first set of legs and the second. Take a tiny wisp of the waterfall wool and felt the wings onto the body by laying the wisp onto the wings and stabbing into the wool, wings and body.

12

Hair
Take a strand of the pink wool top (berries), about 8cm (3^1/$_8$in) long and fold one end over. Lay that end onto the top of the head with the fibres tucked under and the wool top reaching onto the forehead. Felt down on the top with a few stabs first, then fasten the hair on all over but leave the tops soft and hanging down. Cut shorter if you prefer.

Fire Fairy

For me, fire is one of the elements with the most volatility and the most obvious dichotomy: it saves and it destroys.

YOU WILL NEED

WOOL
5g (¹/₆oz) cream standard core/stuffing batts
6g (¹/₅oz) pink South American Merino tops
6g (¹/₅oz) red shimmer NZ Merino batts
7g (¼oz) red-tones Australian Merino tops
3g (¹/₈oz) chestnut bouclé mohair yarn

EXTRAS
1 x 30cm (12in) extra-strong pipe cleaner
1m (39½in) of extra-strong thread
50cm (19¾in) of silky thread.
50cm (19¾in) lengths of brown and red embroidery thread
20 x 15cm (8 x 6in) piece of red tulle with sparkly dots
2 x red feathers

TOOLS
#38 medium felting needle
Sewing needle
PVA glue
Pliers
Scissors
Felting mat

SKILL LEVEL
Crafty beginner
FINISHED SIZE
25cm (10in)
TECHNIQUES USED
Wire wrapping and
needle felting

1

Make a base shape according to the Large Basic Fairy Body instructions on page 16. Note that in Step 4 (page 18) you should use a 16–18cm (6¼–7in) length of pipe cleaner, which you take from the main pipe cleaner once the head is done. Use the red-tones wool tops to wrap the arms by just splitting off a thin strand. Take care not to mess the tops up as they are also used for the smooth main dress – just gently separate a thin strand running along the length. Your fairy should have pink hands and head and red arms.

2

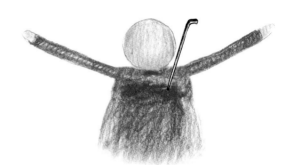

Take the sparkly red shimmer batts (the other red fibre) – they look like a sheet rather than a long strand of fine wool. Flatten the sheet out to approximately 10 x 20cm (4 x 8in) in size. Make a hole in the centre. Bend the arms down and then slip the batts over the fairy's head so that the longer sides are at the front and back. Bend the arms up to hold the wool in place. Use your felting needle to gently stab the wool down on the top part of the fairy, making sure to leave the arms uncovered.

3

Next, take the long red-tones wool top and split off a small strand (this will also be used for the waist tie and hair decoration). Make a hole in the centre of the remaining strands. As before, slip it over the fairy's head. Again, bend the arms up to hold the wool in place, then gently tease the fibres widthways so that they make a cover all around the fairy.

Reserving a little for the hair decoration, tie the remaining red strand around the fairy's waist, just underneath the arms. Pull it tight and secure with a knot. Make sure that the wool on the arms looks the same on each side.

4

Eyes and mouth

Secure your brown eye thread at the back of the head and, using a sewing needle, push the needle all the way through the head to the centre of the face and make a stitch about 2–3mm (1/8in) long for the first eye. If you double the thread, you may only need a couple of stitches back and forth.

Guide the needle below the face to reappear where you will make the second eye and repeat the process. Finish at the back of the head and secure the thread. Use the red embroidery thread and the same sewing technique to make the mouth.

5

Hair

You will work with the bouclé mohair yarn in one continuous strand to make the hair. Felt one end of the bouclé yarn onto the side of the fairy's head, then lay down more yarn at that side of the face and felt it into place. Continue across the forehead to the other side, felting the yarn on as you go – this will frame the face. Next, cover the back of the head. Ensure that you hide the stitches where you secured the eye and mouth threads and that no pink wool shows through.

6

To create a hair bun, start with a new end of yarn. Wind a small amount around one finger to make an olive-sized ball. Felt this onto the top of the fairy's head (do not cut the yarn), then wind more of the yarn around the bun, felting it down as you go. Make it as small or as large as you like.

If you have some yarn left add short lengths to the side of the fairy's head to hang down onto her shoulders.

Use your remaining red-tones wool to wind around the bun. Felt it into place, leaving some wispy ends to hang loose at the side.

7

Wings

Attach the wing feathers by inserting them into the back of the fairy; you may have to wiggle them in a little! You may also need to cut them shorter. Once they are the right length and in the right place, add a dab of glue to secure them and then leave to dry.

Flame Fairy

This little fairy represents more than just fire; she also stands for anything that is known for bright red and orange colours, such as sunrises and sunsets and the bright colours of autumn too!

YOU WILL NEED

WOOL
5g (¹/₆oz) standard core batts
South American Merino tops:
       6g (¹/₅oz) dyed beige
       1g (¹/₂₄oz) natural dark brown
5g (¹/₆oz) dragon NZ Merino batts
3g (¹/₈oz) sunset space-dyed Australian Merino tops
1g (¹/₂₄oz) olive-green Australian Merino batts
2g (¹/₁₂oz) dyed-red curls

EXTRAS
1 x 30cm (12in) extra-strong pipe cleaner
30cm (12in) of raffia
2 x skeleton leaves
1m (39½in) of extra-strong thread

TOOLS
#38 medium felting needle
PVA glue
Pliers
Scissors
Felting mat (optional)

SKILL LEVEL
Crafty beginner
FINISHED SIZE
20cm (8in) long
TECHNIQUES USED
Wire wrapping and a little needle felting

1

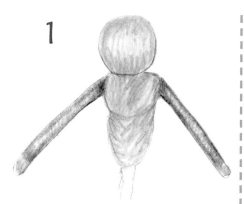

Make a base fairy shape according to the Large Basic Fairy Body instructions on page 16. Note that in Step 4 (page 18) you should use a 16–18cm (6¼–7in) length of pipe cleaner, which you can take from the main pipe cleaner once the head and arms are done. Use the olive-green Australian Merino batts to make the arms.

2

Measure and cut off about 16–18cm (6¼–7in) of the pipe cleaner that extends from the upper body of the fairy. Wrap olive-green wool around the pipe cleaner, leaving about 1cm (³/₈in) exposed on each end. Then take a wisp of dark brown tops and wrap the white end of the pipe cleaner thinly. Bend it inwards and make sure that the bend is covered (as you did for the hands).

3

Continue wrapping the bend; once you have covered about 2cm (¾in), wrap the last wispy ends of the dark brown around the leg like a candy stripe. If you have too much brown tear some off so that you have just enough to make the laces. Repeat on the other side and bend the legs in half. Then bend about 1cm (³/₈in) of the foot in so that you now have little brown-covered feet.

4

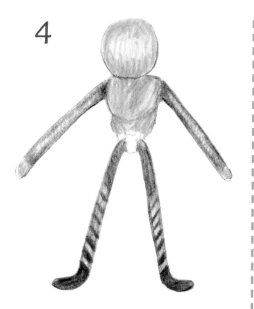

Lay the legs in position below the body – about a head's length away from the head – then take the end of the main body pipe cleaner and wrap it around the legs. Twist it back up and tighten it to secure. You could use some of the pink top to wrap around the legs to secure them further.

5

Take a good pinch of the dragon batts – about the same size as the fairy – keep it flat and tear a hole in the middle. Slip the dragon batts over the head of the fairy so that it reaches just below the waist. If the piece is too large or too thick, take it off and shorten it or make it thinner by

separating parts off it. Use your felting needle to gently stab into the upper body to make the dragon batts a closer fit and to create short sleeves for the fairy. You should not need a felting mat for this as long as you stab at an angle and keep the stabs shallow.

6

Next, take one strand of the sunset wool tops – just a little longer than the fairy itself – and split it in half. Lay one half on the front of the fairy so that the legs are exposed, and the strand reaches over the head. Turn the fairy over and lay the second half on the back, in the same position as for the front. It will look odd as the skirt points the wrong way.

Take the length of raffia and tie it around the waist tightly (the skirt is still covering the fairy's head). Knot the raffia so it is on the side of the fairy.

Pull the skirt down and adjust it by spreading it around the fairy; there will be a small gap on each side. If necessary, shorten the skirt by gently teasing the ends off (take care not to pull it off the fairy). You will want the feet and pretty legs to be visible.

7

Hair

To make the hair, take some of dyed red curls (cut them rather than tearing them apart) and felt them onto one side of the head. Repeat on the other side to frame the face. Once the sides of the face are felted down, cover the rest of the head. Tease the curls sideways to cover more of the head but leave the ends tight.

8

Wings

To attach the wings, take a wisp of wool (dragon NZ or sunset tops) and use it to felt the skeleton leaves onto the back of the fairy, so that she has leaf wings. Alternatively, you could glue them on.

Phoenix

There are many stories from cultures all around the world about what this mythical bird symbolises. It is a symbol of hope and rebirth and gives us the strength to carry on after devastation.

YOU WILL NEED

WOOL
6g (¹/₅oz) orange Mountain sheep batts

1g (¹/₂₄oz) golden-yellow NZ batts

4g (¹/₇oz) natural white core wool batts (Shetland, NZ Merino or South German Merino)

Wisp of black NZ batts

2 x 3g (¹/₈oz) red-orange tone Australian Merino tops about 30cm (12in) long

3g (¹/₈oz) rainbow Australian Merino tops

EXTRAS
1 x 30cm (12in) extra-strong pipe cleaner

TOOLS
#38 medium felting needle

#36 coarse felting needle

Multi-needle tool (optional)

Felting mat

Scissors

SKILL LEVEL
Easy beginner

FINISHED SIZE
25 x 25cm (10 x 10in)

TECHNIQUES USED
Wrapping wire with wool, basic shaping and adding features

1

Cover one end of the pipe cleaner with the golden-yellow wool. Make sure you keep the cover tight and thin and wrap it flat like a ribbon. Cover about 2–3cm (¾–1¼in) in from the end. Bend the pipe cleaner in by about 1cm (³/₈in) and add another covering of golden yellow so that the bent part of the pipe cleaner is covered.

2

Beak

Start to add a layer of orange wool to the pipe cleaner leaving 1cm (³/₈in) of the golden yellow exposed (this will be the beak). Now, cover all the rest of the pipe cleaner with the orange wool, leaving just 2cm (¾in) at the end uncovered.

3

Take all the natural white core wool (leaving a tiny wisp for the eyes) and roll it in on itself into an oval shape. Try to roll it tightly. Felt down the wispy ends to stop the shape from popping open. Felt it into a medium firm oval shape measuring about 6 x 4cm (2½ x 1½in).

4

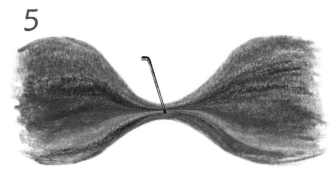

Wings

Take the 30cm (12in) red-orange tone tops and separate out the purple, red and orange parts of the rainbow tops. Make sure that they are slightly shorter; about 25–20cm (8 x 10in) in length. Lay the fibres flat so that the purple is at the base of the red-orange tones. Felt the centre so that it is slightly pinched.

5

Felt the sides so that they become stiffer. If you have a multi-needle tool use this to felt the sides flat from both sides but leave the ends unfelted and wispy. Felt the sides into the shape of wings so that they are rounded at the top and bottom.

6

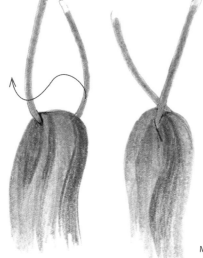

Tail

Tail

Fold the covered pipe cleaner in half, take the other 30cm (12in) length of red-orange wool tops and hook the unfelted tops into the bend (this will become the tail).

Twist the pipe cleaner once to trap the fibres.

7

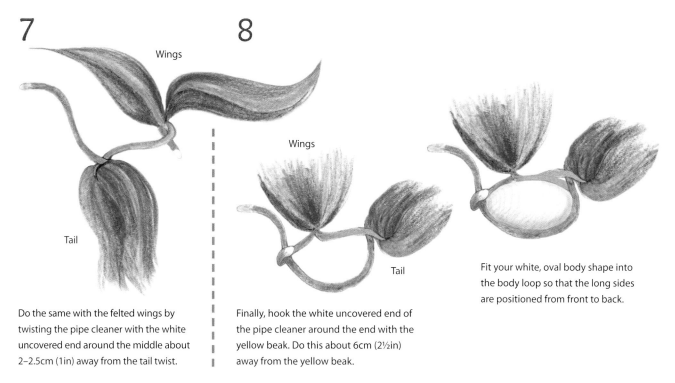

Wings

Tail

Do the same with the felted wings by twisting the pipe cleaner with the white uncovered end around the middle about 2–2.5cm (1in) away from the tail twist.

8

Wings

Tail

Finally, hook the white uncovered end of the pipe cleaner around the end with the yellow beak. Do this about 6cm (2½in) away from the yellow beak.

Fit your white, oval body shape into the body loop so that the long sides are positioned from front to back.

9

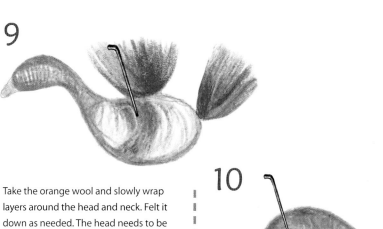

Take the orange wool and slowly wrap layers around the head and neck. Felt it down as needed. The head needs to be about 2–2.5cm (1in) wide, tapering down to the neck, which should be 1.5–2cm (½–¾in). Cover the remaining white body with the orange wool batts. Work with small batches of wool, covering areas rather than continuing to wrap the whole shape. Build up bulk where necessary.

10

Eyes

To make the first eye, take a wisp of the white wool and felt down a disc where one of the eyes will go. Repeat for the other eye, making sure that they are symmetrical. Now, add a smaller black spot on to each of the white discs so that the white still shows clearly around the edges.

11

Mix a little orange with wool with a larger amount of the golden yellow and add the mix to the chest of the bird. Take a tiny wisp of the purple from the rainbow wool tops and felt it on top of the phoenix's head like a fancy hairdo. Adjust the wings and tail by twisting them into the right position. You can shorten them by tearing the wispy ends off. This will also freshen up the look.

Fire Salamander

I always thought that fire salamanders got their name because of the vibrant yellow markings that stand out against the black surface of their skin, but sadly, that is not the case; old folklore has it that people thought they could survive in fire. I like my idea much better!

SKILL LEVEL
Crafty beginner or advanced
FINISHED SIZE
30cm (12in) long
TECHNIQUES USED
Wrapping wire with wool and tape, adding features and other details

YOU WILL NEED
WOOL BATTS
30g (1oz) cream lanolin-rich core wool
10g (1/3oz) dyed-black NZ Merino
3g (1/8oz) golden-yellow NZ Merino

EXTRAS
3 x 36cm (14in) lengths of #22 gauge paper-covered wire
2 x 36cm (14in) lengths of #26 gauge paper-covered wire
Black florist tape
Yellow florist tape (optional)
2 x 8mm black glue-in eyes

TOOLS
#38 medium twisted felting needle
#36 coarse twisted felting needle
Felting mat
PVA glue
Wire cutters or old scissors

1

Toes

Take two of the thinner (#26) wire lengths and cut them into eight equal lengths of 9cm (3½in). You will need four for the front legs and four for the back legs. Take one of the 9cm (3½in) wire lengths and your black florist tape and begin to wrap the tape tightly around the end of the wire, leaving a couple of millimetres at the end uncovered.

Florist tape becomes sticky and pliable when stretched. Work with small lengths of tape, about 8cm (3¹/₈in) or less, making sure the tape overlaps by about 5mm (¹/₈in) and always wrap in the same direction so that you don't unwind layers underneath. If the tape is not sticking everywhere, add a dab of glue and leave it to dry.

2

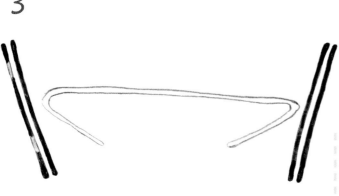

Bend the end of the wire in by 0.5cm (¹/₈in). Cover the bend with more florist tape. Go over it again so that you have added two layers of tape and the thickness is about 3mm (¹/₉in). Then repeat on the other end. The finished length should be 8cm (3¹/₈in). Cover all eight of the 9cm (3½in) wire lengths in the same way. If you have yellow florist tape you could add a couple of thin strips or patches, but this is optional.

3

Feet and legs

For the first set of legs, have your four tape-covered toe sets ready and cut your thicker (#22 gauge) wire so that it measures 22cm (8¾in). Bend each wire end in by 4cm (1½in). Hook the first two toe sets into the 4cm (1½in) bend of the thicker wire. Bend the florist tape covered wire in half, to make four toes. Then, use your fingers or pliers to twist the wire shut around the toes.

4

Take another strip of florist tape and tape around the toes so that you have 1.5cm (½in) long toes and half the lengths of the toes is covered up. Continue covering the foot part and work along the bare wire to cover the twist. Leave about 3–4cm (1¼–1½in) bare in the middle. Repeat for the other three legs, using the remaining toes and the thicker wire. Remember to cut the thicker wire to 22cm (8¾in).

5

Take the final length of thicker (#22 gauge) wire and, using the cream core wool, cover it with one layer of about 1cm (³/₈in). You do not need to bend the ends in. If you find it hard to wrap the wire and the wool slips around, use a dab of glue to secure it, or you could prepare the wire by wrapping it with florist tape first.

Bend one end of the wire in at a right angle at about 5cm (2in) in – this will be the head. Measuring 13cm (5¼in) from the opposite end, wrap a set of legs once, tightly around the wool-covered wire. Add the second set of legs 10cm (4in) from the hind legs.

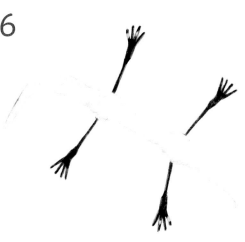

6

Use the core wool to secure the first leg joint by wrapping the wool around it and up towards the head. Repeat for the hind legs. You need to build up bulk on the body so wrap the ends around the middle.

7

The finished size of the body and head at their widest parts will be 4cm (1½in), so the next stage is to work on filling out the head and body using the core wool. Add to the head before moving to the body. Wrap more core wool around the middle between the legs (you can bend them out of the way) and begin to felt down the body and head with your coarse felting needle to firm them up and tuck wispy wool ends away. Be mindful of the wire inside.

8

The wire at the head end of the salamander has not been tucked away, so do this now so that there is no sharp end protruding. Use your pliers to bend the wire inward. This will flatten the nose area, which is also required. Add more wool to the head, especially around the neck and head bend.

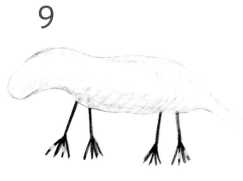

9

Salamanders have broad heads and if you keep wrapping the shape with wool you will make it bigger all around; therefore, you will need to add wool just to specific areas. To do this tear off wisps, rather than strips of wool and lay them on top of one another to make a thicker wad of three or four layers. Add the wads to the side of the head so that the fibres run from front to back and felt them down, working around the edges first, then all over. Repeat on the other side of the head. You have now built up bulk on the sides of the head, keep the top flat.

10

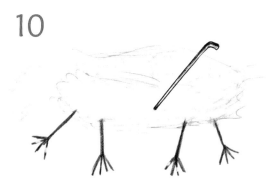

Now that the head is at its finished size, add more wraps around the neck and then work your way down the body. Make sure you do not displace the legs when wrapping the wool: the distance between the two sets of legs should be 10cm (4in). When the body is 4cm (1½in) wide, use long wads of wool to build up the width of the body between the two sets of legs. Make sure the legs come out from the side of the body rather than the underneath. Repeat on the other side.

11

Now that the shape has the right proportions (except the tail), it's time to move on to the black cover. Tease off strands of the black wool and wrap each leg, starting from the toes and moving up to the top of the leg. Using your coarse needle, felt the black wool down, working along the leg to avoid the wire. At the top of the leg, felt the black wool into the cream body. Each leg should be about 1–1.5cm (³⁄₈–½in) wide at the top tapering down to about 0.7–1cm (²⁄₈–³⁄₈in) at the foot part.

You can bend the legs into the right position to get an idea of the overall proportions of the salamander.

12

Tail

Change to your medium felting needle, take a strip of the black wool and, starting at the tip of the tail, tightly wrap about 2cm (¾in) with a layer of black. Felt it down straightaway, and this will secure the black wool. Continue up the tail, adding a tight cover and felting down as you go. If you felt straight into the tail, you may push cream fibres out the other end, so felt the wool down at a shallow angle.

13

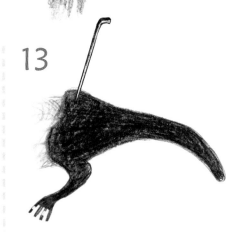

The tail needs to be thicker near the body than at the tip. The body end should be about 3cm (1¼in) wide and the tip about 1–1.5cm (³⁄₈–½in). Add more black wool to build bulk.

14

Continue up the body, but instead of wrapping the whole shape, add patches of black starting on the tummy and working around the main body between the two legs. Keep the cover thin but dense enough to cover the cream wool entirely. Cover the neck and the head in the same way.

15

Eyes

Once the body and head are evenly covered, use your coarse felting needle to make a hole in the side of the head about 3cm (1¼in) away from the tip of the face and only about 1cm (³⁄₈in) from the top of the head. Insert the needle until the thicker part of it sinks into the wool. Insert the pin of the glue-in eye. Then repeat the same process on the other side. If the eyes are symmetrical, add a tiny dab of glue behind them without taking the pins out. Then push them back in and leave to dry.

16

Next, using the black wool, roll a tiny sausage, about 1cm (³⁄₈in) wide and 3cm (1¼in) long. Give it a couple of stabs with your medium felting needle but leave the ends wispy. Make a second sausage of the same size. Felt this over the salamander's eyes like domed covers.

It works best to felt the wispy ends in and then felt into the edge of the sausage rather than felting into the round shape so that you don't flatten it. Then take a tiny wisp of black and lay it over the eye and dome above. Felt down so that the added dome looks more part of the head rather than an add-on. Repeat on the other side.

17

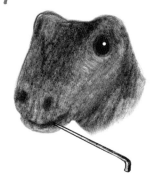

Felt into the area between the two hooded eyes to make it very flat and reduce it in size. This will emphasise the added eye domes. Now felt a line for a mouth and two holes for nostrils with your coarse felting needle. It may be hard to see these features because you are working with black wool, so exaggerate them if needed.

18

Finally, add yellow patches and flecks at random around the whole of the salamander's body. Use your medium felting needle and keep the edges precise. If you make an indentation in the black, felt the black back in so it is the same depth as the yellow.

Smoke Fairy

I always imagine little smoke fairies appearing when I am sitting around a campfire and slithers of smoke escape, seemingly in the shape of a delicate little fairy, released to disappear into the sky.

YOU WILL NEED

WOOL
1g (1/24oz) natural grey Merino tops
1g (1/24oz) Gotland Lamb grey batts
1g (1/24oz) pink Australian Merino batts
Tiny wisps of blue and red for eyes and a mouth (optional)

EXTRAS
1 x 36cm (14in) length of #26 gauge paper-covered wire
1g (1/24oz) ramie tops
30cm (12in) strong thread

TOOLS
#38 medium felting needle
#40 fine felting needle
#42 extra-fine felting needle
Felting mat
PVA glue
Wire cutters or old scissors

SKILL LEVEL
Crafty beginner
FINISHED SIZE
12cm (4¾in)
TECHNIQUES USED
Wrapping wool around wire,
adding features

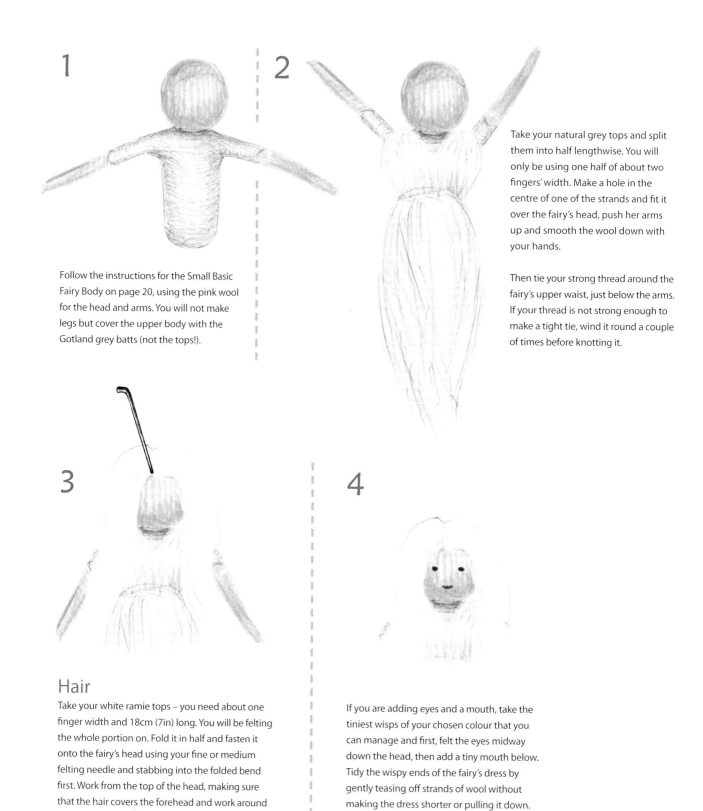

1

Follow the instructions for the Small Basic Fairy Body on page 20, using the pink wool for the head and arms. You will not make legs but cover the upper body with the Gotland grey batts (not the tops!).

2

Take your natural grey tops and split them into half lengthwise. You will only be using one half of about two fingers' width. Make a hole in the centre of one of the strands and fit it over the fairy's head, push her arms up and smooth the wool down with your hands.

Then tie your strong thread around the fairy's upper waist, just below the arms. If your thread is not strong enough to make a tight tie, wind it round a couple of times before knotting it.

3

Hair

Take your white ramie tops – you need about one finger width and 18cm (7in) long. You will be felting the whole portion on. Fold it in half and fasten it onto the fairy's head using your fine or medium felting needle and stabbing into the folded bend first. Work from the top of the head, making sure that the hair covers the forehead and work around the side of the face. Arrange the back and felt it down onto the head leaving most of it hanging freely. Use minimal stabs.

4

If you are adding eyes and a mouth, take the tiniest wisps of your chosen colour that you can manage and first, felt the eyes midway down the head, then add a tiny mouth below. Tidy the wispy ends of the fairy's dress by gently teasing off strands of wool without making the dress shorter or pulling it down.

Frequently Asked Questions

WHEN NEEDLE FELTING, DO YOU FLUFF THINGS UP?

The needle felting process actually does the opposite. You are compressing the wool down and though a finished feltie looks 'fluffy' or soft, comparing it to the un-felted wool it looks a lot less fluffy. It will also become more solid as the fibres tangle together and it will reduce in size

CAN NEEDLES BECOME BLUNT?

Yes, they can, though you have to do an awful lot of felting for this to happen. My needles break before they get blunt.

CAN NEEDLES BREAK?

Yes, they can. I break most of my needles if I hit a wire or pipe cleaner or if I use a fine needle on a fairly solid project. Needles can also break if you put a strain on them going in and out of the wool by making a 'curved' movement. Try and keep your wrist stiff and let the movement come from your arm. Go straight in and straight out.

HOW DO I SHORTEN FEATURES SUCH AS EARS, LEGS, BEAKS ETC?

If you have already attached those parts and you want to shorten them, there are two ways:

1. Stab your needle lengthwise into the part that needs shortening towards the main body of your feltie. Basically, you are continuing to felt the part by going in at a shallow angle therefore reducing the size that way.

2. If your part is already firmly felted and there is little give, use scissors to trim into shape. You can always add wool again to cover any uneven parts that have occurred as a result.

HOW DO I STORE MY WOOL OR FELTED DECORATIONS?

The biggest enemy of all things woolly are clothes moths. These are the little silvery moths that shy away from light (most moths will seek out light). They are only a pest if you have male and female together as the female will find woolly materials to lay her eggs in. When the eggs hatch, the larvae can stay in the wool for up to two and a half years before turning into moths. They can be hard to spot but you will spot the eaten-off ends of wool as they are like a cut edge. The best solution is to have preventative measures in place.

Moths do not like daylight or disturbance so make sure you keep your wool or felties in a light and airy place and move them around occasionally. Or keep them in an airtight bag or container. Put mothballs with a strong scent into the bag or container (you can get cedar balls or more natural sachets that are based on essential oils and lavender).

If you prefer not to use chemicals (moth killing sprays etc) and if you have a large freezer you can kill all moths and larvae by putting the woolly items into it for a couple of days. You can also buy moth traps which attract the male moth (the one that usually flies) and so the female moth (the one that usually hops around the ground) is harmless. The traps need to be replaced regularly.

MY FINISHED FELTIE NEVER LOOKS LIKE THE ONE I HAVE TRIED TO COPY. WHAT AM I DOING WRONG?

Nothing! Needle felting is amazing in that the way that everybody puts their own fingerprint onto their creations and the nature of the wool in its responsiveness and tactility enables you to make something that is truly unique.

Needle felting is different in that respect to sewing, knitting, card making, cross stitch etc. If you are following a pattern, you will likely end up with a carbon copy of the project. Not so in needle felting! This is what I love about it. None of my projects ever looks the same! Enjoy the creative freedom and let your own style develop.

SOMETHING DOES NOT LOOK RIGHT (FACE, SHAPE, PROPORTION ETC) BUT I CAN'T SEE WHAT I NEED TO CHANGE. WHAT SHOULD I DO?

First of all, walk away from it for a bit and then come back with fresh eyes! If you are struggling with the symmetry of a face, for example, look at it in a mirror. That will often give you another perspective and you can see where you have to tweak things. Look at real-life pictures of what you are trying to make for a reality check. We all form images in our mind that are not true to nature.

Sometimes it helps asking a friend who appreciates the work that has gone into your project, to get their constructive feedback. And sometimes you just have to be kind to yourself and stop being over critical or perfectionist!

Resources

UK

THE MAKERSS
www.themakerss.co.uk
info@themakerss.co.uk

For all supplies used in this book and needle felting kits, materials, accessories, tools, tutorials, workshops and talks.

The Makerss
Unit 19
Nailsworth Mills Estate,
Nailsworth, GL6 0BS
Tel 01453 839454

Facebook:
www.facebook.com/themakerss.co.uk
and
www.facebook.com/everyoneamaker

Twitter: @themakerss
Instagram: @themakerss
YouTube: TheMakerssUK for hundreds of tutorials

Australia

MORNING STAR CRAFTS
Tel: +61 (03) 5985 6797
www.morningstarcrafts.com.au

WINTERWOOD TOYS
9 Colman Road
Warranwood
Victoria 3134
Tel: +61 (03) 9879 0426
www.winterwoodtoys.com

Canada

BEAR DANCE CRAFTS
Tel: +1 (250) 353 2220
www.beardancecrafts.com

MAPLEROSE
265 Baker Street
Nelson BC
V1L 4H4
Tel: +1 (250) 352 5729
www.maplerose.ca

USA

A CHILD'S DREAM COME TRUE
214-A Cedar Street
Sandpoint
Idaho 83864
Tel: +1 (208) 255 1664
www.achildsdream.com
info@achildsdream.com

PARADISE FIBERS
225 W. Indiana
Spokane, WA 99205
Tel; +1 (509) 536 7746
www.paradisefibers.com

Acknowledgements

One consistent pillar in my life, come rain or shine, my family! By now they have accepted that I need to write, create and design and I am grateful for their support.

Huge thanks go to Katy Bevan, my editor, who listened, went with my ideas and made it all happen. Her attention to detail and thoroughness is the Ying to my Yang. Her creative heart beats in the same rhythm as mine.

Thank you Martin for being as excited as I am about *Making Fairy Folk* and making yet another dream come true.

Oliver Perrott has captured the magic perfectly in his photography and Saskia Leljak's help with the creative backdrop design and stills was much appreciated.

Lucy Guenot has yet again exceeded all expectations with her beautiful designs and drawings. I will always be in awe, thank you!

Last but not least, I want to thank everyone at *The Makerss* who have supported me during a truly challenging time and who have always found a kind word, lent a helpful hand and who have indulged my need to write books.

Steffi

More books from Hawthorn Press

Making Needle Felted Animals
Over 20 wild, domestic and imaginary creatures
Steffi Stern, Sophie Buckley

Making Needle Felted Animals is an essential guide for anyone interested in the popular craft of needle felting. Whether you are completely new to needle felting or an experienced felter, this book will have something to offer, from precise instruction to creative inspiration.

Written by two authors expert in making and teaching crafts to students of all ages and abilities, instructions are easy to follow and include practical yet creative ideas to fix common mistakes. The projects arise from a genuine love of the natural world and animals, whether they be family pets or wild creatures.

'This book is gorgeous – the animals are so lifelike and appealing – it makes you want to get started straight away.'
Melissa Corkhill, *The Green Parent Magazine*

128pp; 250 x 200mm; paperback; 978-1-907359-46-0

Making Soft Dolls
Simple Waldorf designs to sew and love
Steffi Stern

This book explains why dolls capture the imagination of both children and adults and highlights the power of dolls used for therapeutic purposes. It gives straight-forward instructions for making 10 character dolls and their accessories with clear drawings and templates. It also includes a guide to buying your materials and upcycling materials you already own. A lovingly hand-made doll makes the perfect present and these dolls are easy to make and will be much loved for generations.

128pp; 250 x 200mm; paperback; 978-1-912480-0-50

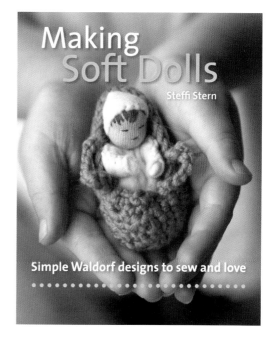

Ordering Books

If you have difficulties ordering Hawthorn Press books from a bookshop, you can order direct from our website www.hawthornpress.com, or from our UK distributor:
BookSource, 50 Cambuslang Road, Glasgow, G32 8NB
Tel: (0845) 370 0063   Email: orders@booksource.net.

Details of our overseas distributors can be found on our website.

Hawthorn Press
www.hawthornpress.com